HikingTrails
of
Southwestern
Colorado

A Guide to Colorado's
Most Spectacular Mountain Peaks
in the San Juan and
Uncompahgre National Forests

HikingTrails
of
Southwestern
Colorado

Paul Pixler

PRUETT **P** *PUBLISHING COMPANY*
Boulder, Colorado

First Edition

7   8   9

Printed in the United States of America

Library of Congress Cataloging in Publication Data

Pixler, Paul, 1920-
   Hiking trails of Southwestern Colorado.

   1. Hiking—Colorado—San Juan National Forest—
Guide-books. 2. San Juan National Forest (Colo.)—
Guide-books. I. Title.
GV199.42.C62S266   917.88'25   81-5227
ISBN 0-87108-579-8 (pbk.)   AACR2

Dedicated to:

My wife, Bettie, and the hikers who have
accompanied me on many of these trails:
Adeline Becay, John Fleming, Charlotte
Hammond, Audine Hayden, Anne Pixler, Glenn
Phillips, Ed and Winnie Sinden, Diane Skinner,
and Marianna Stanley.

Contents

1: Introduction   1

2: Hikes Near Durango   15
Animas City Mountain   15
Hogsback   20
Barnroof Point   22
Dry Creek to Durango   25
Raider Ridge   27
Twin Buttes   31
Perins Peak   34

3: Hikes Up and On Missionary Ridge   41
Haflin Creek   41
Wallace Lake   44
Mountain View Crest   46
Burnt Timber Trail   52
Red Creek Trail   55
Shearer Creek   59

4: La Plata Mountain Climbs   63
Kennebec Pass—Taylor Lake   63
Silver Mountain   67
Tomahawk Basin—Diorite Peak   71
Centennial Peak and Sharkstooth   74
Hesperus Mountain   79
Parrott Peak   82
Gibbs Peak   85

5: Hikes Between Durango and Silverton 89

Hermosa Trail   89
Mitchell Lakes   92
Goulding Creek   95
Elbert Creek   98
Four Base Lake   101
Molas Trail   103
Purgatory Trail   106
Potato (Spud) Lake   109
Potato Hill (Spud) Mountain   113
Engineer Mountain   115
Grizzly Peak   119
Jura Knob   124
(Coal Creek, Deer Creek)
Sultan—Grand Turk   128
Crater Lake—Twilight Peaks   131
Snowdon Peak   136
Graysill Mountain—Grayrock Peak   140
Hermosa Peak   143

6: Hikes Out of Silverton 147

South Mineral Creek—Cascade   147
Lake Hope   154
Ice Lakes   157
Clear Lake   162
Kendall Mountain   165
Deer Park Trail—Whitehead Peak   168
Highland Mary Lakes   172
Continental Divide   176
Silver Lake   180

7: The Area Fourteeners 183

Mount Sneffels   185
Wilson Peak   190
Handies Peak   196
Red Cloud and Sunshine   200
Uncompahgre Peak,
Matterhorn, Wetterhorn   204

Index   213

CHAPTER 1

Introduction

Why hike in southwestern Colorado? Because hiking is great fun and a healthy activity; because there is hardly a better place on earth to hike than southwestern Colorado. It offers a variety of terrain and altitude on large amounts of public land, an excellent and varied climate, and exceptionally beautiful scenery.

The lower altitudes can be hiked typically from April through November, with some hiking, especially when aided by snowshoes, available the rest of the year. Altitudes up to 10,000 feet can be hiked without special snow equipment typically from late May to early November if you do not go into heavily shaded areas. Above 10,000 feet, the season is shorter, typically late June until early fall snows, which usually are not permanent until after the middle of October or even later, depending on the particular year and the altitude.

The area offers vast hiking opportunities; this guidebook covers much of the best of it, but it cannot cover all of it. The hikes selected for inclusion here use Durango and Silverton as the starting points for directions. All of the hikes are near these two towns and include several spots between the two. It may be possible at a later date to publish another guide covering other options in this part of the state.

The hikes are planned for half-day and full-day trips. This is not a backpacker's book, although some of the trails are useful for that if anyone wants to take them at a very leisurely pace. A few of the hikes are best handled by driving in the day before the hike and car camping. But for all of the trips in this book, only a day pack is needed. With its lighter weight, it is a more pleasant burden.

The hikes described range from easy to difficult, from short to long, from relatively level to some long climbs. All types of hikers should be able to find something to suit their own tastes. None of the climbs require any technical gear or skills. Some places pose a degree of danger, but these only require carefulness. Cliff edges, for example, should always be approached cautiously, but they frequently furnish breathtaking views and are safe to anyone exercising due care. Of course, you should make sure that the cliff edge is not cracking away before trusting it.

Most of the hikes are exclusively on public land. A few National Forest trails cross private land, and the Forest Service has made proper arrangements with owners. Occasionally public and private lands are so intermixed that boundaries cannot be identified. This is particularly true of small patented mining claims in mineralized areas as, e.g., in some spots of La Plata Canyon. Where private property boundaries are identifiable due care for private rights should be exercised as appropriate anywhere, whether in the mountains or in town.

THE HEADINGS

At the beginning of each hike description, I have given seven items in tabular form to aid the hiker in judging key issues to suit his interests. Some explanation of these items is due.

After the *name* of the hike comes the *distance*. This is identified as to one way or round trip. It is difficult to be accurate on distances, but they should give some help in estimating time involved; however, this will vary from person to person, from steep uphill to flat or downhill, and from smooth to rough. The average hiker takes about twice as long to go up steep terrain as to descend. The higher the altitude, the greater will be the differential.

Elevations are given for the starting and highest points, total *elevation gain* is also listed. This gives some clue to difficulty and steepness when compared to distance. Usually, altitude gain is the simple difference between starting point and high point, but in some cases, where an intervening loss must be regained, total gain will be more. The level of difficulty depends on altitude to be

The north sheer face of Uncompahgre Peak.

climbed and on steepness and roughness. The rating system takes all of these into consideration. Also, a one-thousand-foot climb that begins at 6,000 feet is much easier than a one-thousand-foot climb that starts at 13,000 feet.

Higher altitudes are in themselves a hazard to some people. To those who live in Durango or Silverton or similar elevations and who are in good health and are used to some exercise, any altitude in Colorado should pose no special problem. People coming into this area from low altitudes may experience some difficulty. Some visitors are breathless even in town.

Altitude affects you in several ways, most of which are dependent on the lowered atmospheric pressure and a resulting lower oxygen content per breath. If you find yourself panting at or below 10,000 feet with very little effort expended, you are not ready for any long hikes described here. Also, people with a history of heart problems or high blood pressure should probably consider only the easier and lower hikes.

Acclimatization to high altitude seems to be basically an increase in red blood cell count, which makes for a more efficient use of the available oxygen in the thinner air. People from lower altitudes who have done some sustained (aerobic) exercise may have

3

a higher red blood cell count and may not be as likely to have altitude problems in Colorado; others may help the situation by staying a couple of days or more at altitudes of 5,000 to 8,000 feet before climbing above 11,000 feet.

Some people even in apparent good health may have some problems. Besides shortness of breath, headaches can come on. My wife, who has lived at 6,500 feet a number of years, still can tell when we reach 10,000 feet in a car by the onset of a headache. Some may experience light-headedness or an upset digestive system. If any of these symptoms become severe, it is a good idea to get down to a lower altitude quickly to recover from "altitude sickness." Often these symptoms will subside with a good rest and a slower pace so that the hike can be continued satisfactorily. The percentage of people who have severe problems is small, so this word of caution should not deter most people in good health from taking any of these hikes. For most, high-altitude hiking can be an exhilarating experience, especially when they top their first peak and look down with awe on the other side. It is a moment of achievement and beauty that puts a new dimension into living!

Each of the hikes is rated for level of difficulty. The *ratings* used are easy, moderate, difficult, and hard. Any usage of terms like these is relative to the condition and experience of each hiker, so much so that some people might regard any of these hikes easy, while someone else might regard most of them hard.

I am giving the ratings based on persons in reasonably good health and with at least a minimum level of experience with hikes of a few miles length. The ratings should fit a wide range of age groups, say ten years to seventy years or more of both sexes. Whether you agree with any ratings after trying some of these hikes will depend mostly on your physical condition. Seasoned mountain hikers are likely to think of these grades a notch or two too easy. So adjust them up or down to fit your own experience. A couple of hikes on these routes should set your proper interpretation of them.

Several factors are included in arriving at the ratings; these are length of the hike, altitude gain, difficulty in following the route, and difficulty in getting over the route. Of these, two are most important. First is altitude gain. Practically all of these hikes include some climbing. This makes the hike much more interesting, especially if a summit with good views is attained and if the trail takes you through changing climatic zones. Altitude gain can bring more difficulty than just increased effort, however. If can bring "altitude sickness," which will require slowing down a bit.

4

The Animas Canyon and the Grenadier Range from the Molas Trail.

Mostly, climbing should be fun and a way to get good exercise; the fun comes through interesting observations (of vegetation, animals, rocks, waterfalls, babbling brooks, and mountains), a sense of accomplishment, and companionship. But those who are in good physical condition are likely to enjoy it more than others.

The most important problem in the ratings has to do with the actual surface to be traversed. There is a great deal of difference between a smooth trail and a rocky one. None of the hikes described here are technical climbs involving ropes or other special equipment, but some involve talus and some rock scrambling.

Talus, or loose rock that varies roughly from eight inches to two feet in size, is typical at altitudes above timberline and often slightly below it. Talus areas may vary from being nearly flat to being so steep that they are ready to slide with any loosening. The slide point is called the angle of repose. When the talus is this steep, great care is necessary to avoid starting a slide or even the fall of a single rock. This can endanger yourself, but it is especially hazardous for any companions below you.

The most common problem with talus is not from falling rocks but just that it is more difficult to walk on. With some experience, you can walk on it almost as fast as on smooth ground; it takes concentration on each step to see that the rock about to be stepped on is firmly placed. Without this, you are likely to turn an ankle or jab a shin or ankle with a sharp-edged rock.

Rock scrambling means using the hands as well as the feet to climb over rocks. Many climbs have some of this, especially near the top. It can be fun and offer variety to a hike. It can get you over near-vertical obstacles and on to higher glory.

Talus and rock scrambling problems, unless they are minor, quickly increase the level of difficulty given in the ratings.

Time allowed is estimated for an average hiker, but, of course, there is no average hiker; so the times must be treated as guidelines, not fixed truths. Some will hike faster and some slower than that given, even though a range is estimated. The times given do not allow for time used in driving to or from trail heads. This must be estimated extra. Also, times given are for actual hiking and short breath-catching stops. If you want to take long stops for pictures, lunch, a nap on a sunny hillside, or just to drink in the beauty or to talk with a companion, these should be added to the estimates.

A word about rest stops is appropriate. At higher altitudes in steep areas, almost everyone has to rest occasionally. When you are working hard, short rests of thirty seconds to a minute and a half are best. These can be frequent if necessary. Long rests of five to twenty minutes can be devastating. In the first place, they increase the total hiking time an amazing amount, but more importantly, they make you lose your "second wind." This makes it difficult to get going again and to get up to the same pace that you were maintaining earlier with relative ease. It slows down the whole cardiovascular system and slows the efficiency that you have previously attained in your climbing muscles. You have to get your second wind all over again.

Maps can be a big help. People who are used to hiking in the eastern United States, such as along the Appalachian Trail, may not need maps there due to the heavy traffic and the well-defined trails marked with frequent cairns. Hiking in Colorado, where altitudes are higher, where terrain and climate change more, and where the whole area is so much more vast, is a much different experience.

The maps given in this book are for describing the hike, but on longer hkes, other maps are useful for showing more of the surrounding territory. Two kinds of maps are typically listed in the headings. The national forest maps show roughly where the trails go. They are limited, however, due to their small scale and their lack of altitude gradations.

The U.S. Geological Survey maps give much more detail. The 7½-minute series of quad maps show topographical gradations of 40 feet from one line to the next, with 200-foot lines heavier to delineate the larger gradations. Even these maps cannot show small cliffs that can cause significant detours from straight-line hiking. While many of the hikes are over established trails, some are not, and even some of the trails have breaks in them due to inadequate maintenance; hiking at this point is "bushwhacking," i.e., finding your own way. This may literally be through the bushes, or it may be over rocks or through trees. This can add its own challenge. The hike descriptions attempt to lead you through these areas without difficulty.

National forest maps can be obtained through forest head-quarters offices and ranger stations. Occasionally, you can find them in sporting goods stores. The topo maps are carried by several sporting goods stores, especially those that carry hiking and climbing gear. Sometimes they can be found in magazine stores and in libraries.

Looking up from the Cascade Trail through timber to Engineer Mt.

THE WEATHER

Hikers in higher altitudes in the Rockies must always be aware of the weather. It can change from beautiful to dangerous very quickly. This is especially true from June to early September, when afternoon thunderstorms are frequent. During this period, it is better to plan to reach the highest altitude in your hike by noon if possible. These storms can be severe, even though short-lived. They can bring wind, cold, rain, and small hail, depending on the particular storm. The greatest hazard, however, is lightning. It is high-voltage static electricity and can kill or maim in a split second. High points where the charged cloud is closest are the strike points. This makes high or isolated peaks especially vulnerable. But tall trees below the peak are also frequent targets.

Any dark cloud nearby in the summer should be suspect, even if it is small. There are additional signs of an imminent lightning flash. If you are on or near a high point above surrounding territory and you hear a buzzing in the rocks, or if the hair on your arms or legs or neck, and even on your head, begins to try to stand up, you're in prime territory; get down to lower levels as fast as possible. Also, if you seek shelter from rain under a tree, make it a tree lower than others nearby.

Lightning is the worst danger from storms, but not the only one. Rocks that call for scrambling can be very slick when they get wet. Lichens on them increase this problem. When I climbed El Diente recently, it began drizzling just after our party started down from the top; the rocks are near-vertical and are very irregular in this area. I slipped on one that would have held easily when dry. Though I fell only three feet, that led to an edge where there was another drop followed by another and another. Fortunately, two companions were at the edge of the first one and stopped me before I could go to the next drop. Though embarrassing, it served as a reminder to become more cautious, but it could have been disastrous.

In the high country, it can snow any month of the year, although significant amounts are rare in the summer. Only a light coating, however, slickens up the footholds and handholds.

Another danger from rainstorms is hypothermia. This is a condition in which the core body temperature begins to drop below normal. Cold fingers and toes are uncomfortable, but a cold body core is highly dangerous. Soaked clothes and some wind can bring this on quickly, even in July. When you begin to shiver violently, hypothermia is starting. Companions must come to the rescue and furnish heat immediately, because the victim soon becomes disoriented and does not recognize his danger. Fires are usually out of the question because of the rain. Extra clothing will help if the situation is not too bad; also, a faster pace can help when it can be done. However, in more severe cases, skin-to-skin body heat transfer is likely to be the only answer.

EMERGENCIES

It is best when hiking in hazardous backcountry to go in parties of not less than three. If one falls and is hurt to the point of not being able to go on, another can stay with that person while the third goes for help. The one who stays should administer first aid and keep the injured person as warm and comfortable as possible. This will call for a fire if it becomes cold or dark. The patient should also be given plenty of fluids, for dehydration takes place rapidly at high altitudes. Dehydration of an injured person adds to the danger as well as to the discomfort.

One of the most frequent hazards is the possibility of getting lost. While I have written this guide with a great deal of care to prevent this from happening, there is no guarantee against it. A slightly different interpretation of the text than intended can sometimes cause trouble. Also, it is possible that the text has errors, although I have tried hard to prevent this.

The best approach is not to get lost. Several things help. Keep the hiking group fairly close together. Each person should take note of prominent features in the area as guideposts, just in case. Also, a compass is a good idea; learn how to read and use it. It can be used in connection with the trail map.

Suppose you do get lost? Don't panic. Think through where you were just before getting lost, and take your bearings from this. Usually, the trail map should show you enough to keep drainages sorted out to the point where you can get back to the one you came up. Study over any prominent peaks, trees, or rocks that you remember seeing before, and reorient from them. Check your compass. Check the sky for direction. The sun and the moon are great guides when available. On a starry night with

9

no moon, the Big Dipper is your clue. The North Star is straight out from the lip of the Dipper. It is a faint star; if you can't find it, the lip star of the Dipper itself will approximate north, but it varies its position during the night. The North Star does not.

Rock Scrambling.

Any drainage will always eventually lead to civilization; so you can always follow down the nearest one if all else fails. This, however, has its drawbacks. First, it may be a long way out. Second, drainages have their own difficulties: cliffs or waterfalls must be skirted; cliff walls next to the stream may cause you to walk in the water or cross the stream frequently; brush and mud near the creek don't help. If you know that you are a considerable distance from a road, house, or camp, and if you are hopelessly lost, the best answer is to build a fire and make yourself as comfortable as possible while awaiting rescue.

This treatment of emergencies and hazards may give the impression that hiking in southwestern Colorado is highly dangerous, only to be undertaken by the experienced and the foolhardy; this is far from the truth. It is most likely to be highly enjoyable, even ecstatically so, if a few proper precautions are taken. In thirteen years of hiking and leading hiking groups in

10

this area, I have only had to manage one injury of consequence. This was a broken wrist that was sustained when a fellow hiker caught his toe on a small rock. The place was nearly flat—not recognizably more dangerous than a city street curb. It was the freak combination of circumstances that could have happened anywhere. So get yourself properly prepared, and head for the hills!

EQUIPMENT

A part of preparation is proper equipment. There are a number of good manuals about this subject, so I will treat it quite briefly.

Any hiker's equipment starts with shoes. They should be comfortable and large enough, both in length and width, especially across the toes. The size should allow for fairly thick socks, or even two pair—one thin pair and a second thicker pair. Two pair, if one is thin and a bit slick, can reduce friction and blisters. Also, the risk of blisters, if you are prone to them, can be reduced by lubricating the skin at wear points with Vaseline or even oleo.

The best insurance against blisters is the right shoe. Many people think that you need a heavy and expensive hiking boot. The only real requirements are comfort and adequate protection. Lighter-weight boots with rugged treaded soles are usually adequate and will not tire you as much as heavier boots. The pair I enjoyed most and that gave me no blister problems were logger's boots. They had Vibram soles, good flexibility, good toe width, and a steel protective cover over the toes that prevents leather shrinkage as well as battering injuries. Actually, tennis or jogging shoes are fine for the easy, well-worn trails where the surface is not very rocky or rough.

A day pack will be necessary for carrying food, extra clothing, a first-aid kit, water, and a camera. There are many good ones. Any day pack should be waterproof to protect its contents.

Coats, jackets, sweaters, and T-shirts are all appropriate to consider for the upper body. Even in hot weather, be sure to have enough along if you are going to go up to any significant altitude. Eighty-five-degree weather can quickly change to fifty degrees or lower with a cold wind when you climb. For the upper body, layers for varying temperatures and windchill factors are

11

best. At least one layer should be wool, for it is warm and can insulate even when wet. Down will not do any good when wet, though it is lightweight and very good when dry. There should always be a windbreaker jacket in your supply; even just a thin plastic one can be a major help. Wind seeping through sweaty or rain-soaked clothes can turn them into a deep-freeze quickly. Actually, wind is not typical in southwestern Colorado even on high peaks, but it can come up strongly without much warning. You should also have rain gear. This can be a lightweight poncho or a rain suit; even a large garbage bag will do in an emergency.

I like long pants for most hiking, though some of my friends like shorts in warm weather. In the first place, I sunburn quite easily and like to keep the least amount of skin exposed. Another important consideration against shorts is brush, and even briars, which can scratch exposed legs unmercifully.

Snowshoeing.

Usually, you should also take along a warm cap capable of covering the ears, since nearly half of lost body heat can escape through the head. A pair of gloves should be included, too—they are needed at times for warmth but are often useful in rock scrambling as protection against abrasion of the skin.

There should be at least one first-aid kit in any hiking group. It should include Band-Aids, moleskin (for foot blisters), water purifier, aspirin, an Ace bandage, gauze, a sunscreen lotion, some *dry* matches, a compass, and a flashlight. Each person who cannot whistle naturally should carry a whistle to help when lost.

I like to carry a piece of one-eighth-inch nylon rope. It can be used for repairs on equipment, for shoelaces, for a makeshift arm sling, and untold other things. The sunscreen should be used regularly, for the sun burns more quickly at higher altitudes.

Finally, if you are a photographer, by all means have your camera along and handy. A pair of lightweight binoculars is often useful, too.

On trips of any significant length, be sure to take a canteen of water and usually some food. If you are a fisherman, you will want to carry fishing gear on the appropriate trips.

Overlooking Animas Valley from Animas Mountain.

CHAPTER 2

Hikes near Durango

Animas City Mountain

Distance: 5 miles (round trip)
Starting Elevation: 6,680 feet
Elevation Gain: 1,481 feet
High Point: 8,161 feet
Rating: Easy
Time Allowed: 3.5 to 4 hours
Maps: 7½ ' Durango East
San Juan National Forest

This is an easy half-day hike near Durango. It is a good hike at any time of year, but it is especially appealing when the higher country is too deeply covered with snow for good hiking. This means November to June. Through the middle of the winter there is usually plenty of snow even on Animas Mountain. At that time, this becomes good territory for snowshoeing and ski touring. When the snow is deep, the elk come down to winter at this level. I have hiked this mountain many many times; during the period from December to May I almost always see elk and occasionally a deer. Sometimes I have seen as many as two dozen elk. They are

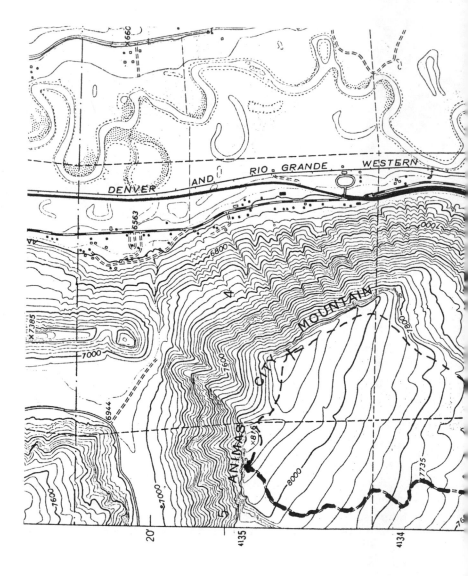

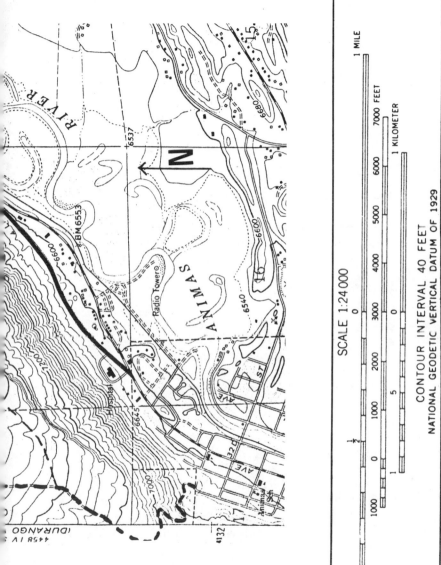

SCALE 1:24 000

CONTOUR INTERVAL 40 FEET
NATIONAL GEODETIC VERTICAL DATUM OF 1929

17

usually about three-fourths of the way to the top. On snowy, winter days they may often be seen browsing on the steep, but warm, southeast side.

To do this hike, take Thirty-Second Street west of Main Street in Durango to its end on West Fourth Avenue. Turn right here, and go to the end of the street (only about two blocks). Parking space is not generous here, but you can usually find room for a car. Immediately above you at this point is an electrical substation. On its north side, take the old four-wheel-drive road steeply up the hill to the west. The road continues to climb steeply for .4 mile; at the third switchback there is a nice view down over Durango. Here you will also be at the top of the rimrock that characterizes all sides of this mountain. From this point to the top, the hike follows a mild rise except for a couple of short spots. The old road goes all the way to the north end of the mountain, where you will have a fine view north up the Falls Creek valley and west across a valley to the La Plata Mountains.

The time and distance given above presuppose your returning down the same road. But the actual highest point lies about a half mile east of here. If you have time, this is a welcome addition to the hike. The northeast point of the mountain looks down into the Animas Valley and shows the torturous winding of the river amid pastures populated with horses and cattle. There are also some old turns of the river now bypassed and disconnected. These usually have water in them from the spring snow melt. The total scene is peaceful and pastoral in contrast to so many rugged mountain views around Durango.

The top of Animas Mountain is covered with large Ponderosa pine. If you have gone to the northeast corner, it is not difficult for you to return down through the woods along the east rim. This rim is precipitous, and there are only a few places to break through it safely. So I suggest that you head south with a little bias to the west. There is a four-wheel-drive trail coming up the east side of the mountain. If you find it, follow it on down; it will eventually join the original road only a half mile above your parking spot. If you do not strike this road, keep angling a bit to the west, and you will reach the original road a little higher up.

For those who like to keep their legs in good climbing form even in winter, I recommend climbing Animas Mountain from the southeast side. Because of the angle of exposure, snow does not usually stay long here.

18

For this approach, park in the Community Hospital parking lot. It is located just west of Highway 550 at the north end of Durango. From the northwest corner of the parking area, start climbing north and west. There is no trail, but there are plenty of open spaces in the brush and low trees. The more west you climb, the steeper it becomes; the more north you hike, the more you can ameliorate the steepness. A large elk population often winters in this steep area. The finest bull elk portrait I have ever taken was photographed in this area. About three-fourths of the way up to the rim is a nice large shelf. This is a good place to find deer and elk if you have not found them lower down. At one time I spotted a large herd here with an unusual albino elk.

Elk on Animas Mountain in the winter.

Hogsback

Distance: 2 miles (round trip)
Starting Elevation: 6,641 feet
Elevation Gain: 843 feet
High Point: 7,484 feet
Rating: Easy, except last 200 yards.
Time allowed: 1¼ hours
Maps: 7½' Durango West

This is a close hiking area to Durango, for it comes right up to the western city limits. There are many bypaths in the shale hills here that make good evening or leisurely Sunday afternoon strolling or good winter snowshoeing and ski touring. There is enough altitude gain to provide an opportunity to look down on Durango and up to Perins Peak. Deer live in these hills year-round; in winter, with deep snow, there are elk. I once saw a herd of over thirty elk on a quick Saturday morning snowshoe trip.

More than one square mile of this area is worth exploring. Much of it is private property, but the present owner does not restrict hikers—only motorcycles and snowmobiles. The interest here has been damaged somewhat for hiking in the last year by the opening of a sanitary land fill in a valley, but there is still a lot of good hiking in spite of it.

The hike described here is the most challenging and most rewarding in this area. There are several ways to start—one of my favorites is off the west end of Leyden Street. It is the same starting point as described for Perins Peak.

Take Main Street in Durango to Twenty-Second and turn west. Twenty-Second angles to the top of Crestview Mesa, where it becomes Mountview Parkway. Follow this to Glenisle and turn south (left) to its end on Kearney. Start hiking here by climbing over a little earth barrier and crossing the stream (usually dry). Here the route is steeply uphill through oak brush. There are two or three paths through the brush; they are twisting but better than a route through the thickest places. At the top of a hundred-foot climb the going is much easier, for here is a good foot and motorcycle trail leading west toward the Hogsback. Follow this a quarter mile to the top of the first rise where you should find a trail that leads southwest and that winds around a bit. It goes generally west along the ridge and eventually steeply north and finally west to the top of Hogsback. The last 300 yards provide more than half of the altitude gain on this hike. It is a good practice hike for the interested hikers who aspire to higher things.

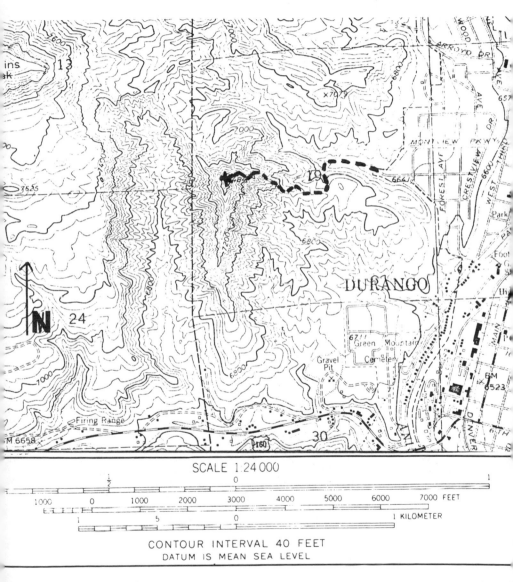

SCALE 1:24 000

CONTOUR INTERVAL 40 FEET
DATUM IS MEAN SEA LEVEL

This hill is known locally as the Hogsback, but it does not fit the geologist's definition of the term. It is all Mancos shale (a gray, flaky soil, usually soft at the surface) except at the top, where it is capped with sandstone.

The last bit of this hike is a tight squeeze, and you must be careful not to slip, lest you take a steep, unscheduled glissade in the shale for about 150 feet. The steep part is on your left. The right side is brush; it is a good idea to hold on to the brush. On the top there is a nice single slab of sandstone that becomes your reward for huffing and puffing to the top. This slab makes a good place to lie down and rest or to sit and study the city below.

The return should be made on the same route as the approach, at least down the steep part. On the return, after the hazardous part at the top, the loose shale that was so hard to climb becomes an asset, for you can have fun shuffling, almost skiing, down the steep part.

Barnroof Point

Distance: 5 miles (round trip)
Starting Elevation: 6,940 feet
Elevation Gain: 1,783 feet
High Point: 8,723 feet
Rating: Moderate
Time Allowed: 2½ to 3½ hours
Maps: 7½ ' Durango West
San Juan National Forest

Barnroof Point is on Colorado Wildlife and Bureau of Land Management property, but it shows on the forest service map. The lower part of the south and southwest sides is private property. It is a good place to see deer anytime of year and elk from November to May, depending on snow depths higher up. Also, the top affords one of the best views of the east side of the La Platas.

Barnroof is heavily vegetated, especially with Ponderosa pine and oak brush. The brush is from knee-high to ten or twelve feet. It can be a real thicket and hard to get through. Since part of this hike will require bushwhacking, you need to be aware of the oak brush problem. Staying near the east and north sides of the mountain will help you avoid most of this.

Barnroof is a low mountain east of the La Platas. It is interesting in that it stands as a single peak with valleys on all sides. This makes it a nice climb for presenting good views of surrounding territory.

To start the hike, go west of Durango on Highway 160 three and one-half miles to a right turn on Lightner Creek Road. Follow it one mile north to where it turns sharply left and crosses Dry Fork. Instead of turning, go straight ahead through a gate. Park just inside.

Begin hiking west across the creek, usually a very small stream, and up the other side. In 200 yards, you should strike an old road. Take this up the east side, going north to its termination in .7 mile. Unfortunately, it stops short of reaching the top of the steep side, so you will have to scramble up about twenty feet. Once on this rim, it will be easy going most of the way. Hike just back of the rim in a northerly direction and eventually in a northwest direction one and one-fourth miles to the top. By staying near the rim, you do not encounter much of the brush. Also, there will be many fine views of the valleys below and the peaks beyond. However, big-game animals are more likely to be back farther, even in the brush.

Just before reaching the top, you will find some interesting trenches that appear to have been caused by some ancient geological disturbances.

The view of the La Platas from the high point, the northwest corner, is great. With a deep valley between, foothills sweep upward to the rocky high peaks, forming a majestic view.

The easiest return is by the approach route, but brave souls may want to vary from that. If so, head south one-half to one mile; then veer east to strike the descent road back to the parking area. This route passes through big pines, an occasional meadow, and, unfortunately, brush thickets. These can be crossed with patience, but they are a nuisance. Perhaps you will see deer and/or an elk this way.

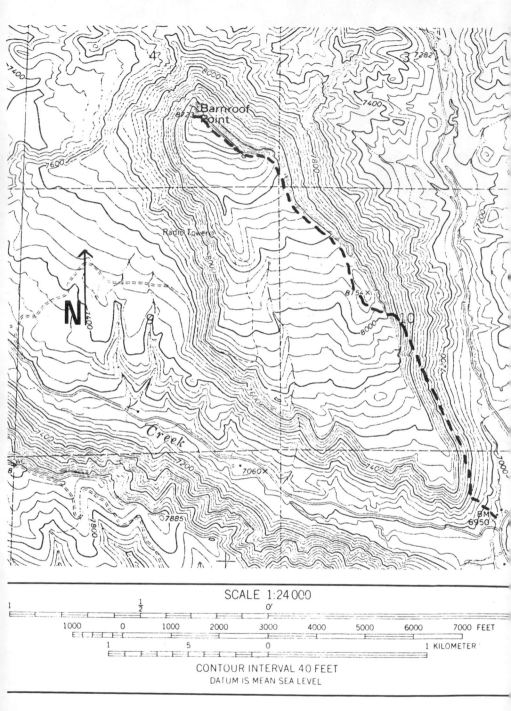

SCALE 1:24 000

CONTOUR INTERVAL 40 FEET
DATUM IS MEAN SEA LEVEL

24

Dry Creek to Durango

Distance: 5 miles (one way)
Starting Elevation: 7,280 feet
Elevation Gain: 400 feet
High Point: 7,680 feet
Rating: Easy
Time Allowed: 2 to 3 hours
Maps: 7½' Durango West
      San Juan National Forest

This is an easy afternoon hike near Durango. Although it is on the forest service map, the route lies just outside the national forest boundary and traverses Colorado Wildlife property, a little Bureau of Land Management territory, and, for the last mile, private property. The private property makes it subject to possible closure, but it is a nice hike while available.

This hike involves having transportation available at both ends. It is routed west to east, since this only involves 400 feet of altitude gain; east to west presents 1,000 feet of gain.

As a wildlife feeding spot, this area offers good opportunities to see big game. Deer roam here year-round; elk are here from the early snows until spring, roughly November to April. You may also see bear here from time to time, and, on occasion, wild turkey. Hunting is permitted in season. If the high country is snowed in early enough, hunting for both deer and elk can be very good here.

To reach the hiking route, drive west of Durango three and one-half miles to a right turn on Lightner Creek Road. Follow it one mile north to where it makes a sharp turn left and crosses Dry Fork. Instead of turning, go straight ahead through a gate. This puts you into the Wildlife area. Continue two miles north to where the road splits; take the right side for another quarter mile to a wire gate. Turn right, and go downhill in front of the gate to a parking area. The hike begins here; it ends at the west end of Clovis Street in Durango, where another car can be parked.

From the western parking spot, start hiking east. The first task is to cross Dry Fork; it usually is a small stream and can easily be jumped. Beyond the creek bank lies a nice meadow with a gently rising slope. Hike toward the east and a little north up this meadow; along its north side, just in the edge of the timber, you should find the remains of an old road. You follow it essentially all the way into Durango. The route rises now in less than a mile to its highest point in some big Ponderosa pines. Off to the right and high above is the sharp point of the north end of the Perins Peak massif. From here on it is downhill, alternating between tall pines and open meadows. The meadow grasses are sometimes high enough to obscure the trail. In such cases, stay near the low point on the north side of the ditch. At three and one-half miles you will pass the remains of some old ranch buildings with a nice cattail pond on the right followed by another meadow. The next meadow beyond that is usually quite marshy; here it is best to cross to the south side. At four miles, you will come to a fence with steel steps over it. You are now on a better road and have to hike one mile to Clovis on private property; so you should stay on the road.

This area is good in the winter for snowshoeing and ski touring. In fact, Dry Creek valley at the west end is quite popular for ski touring since it is not at all steep.

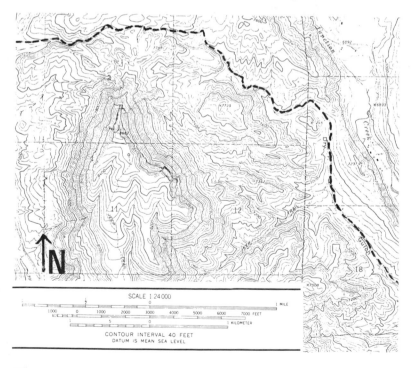

SCALE 1:24 000

CONTOUR INTERVAL 40 FEET
DATUM IS MEAN SEA LEVEL

Raider Ridge

Distance: 1 mile (round trip)
Starting Elevation: 7,000 feet
Elevation Gain: 450 feet
High Point: 7,450 feet
Rating: Easy
Time Allowed: 1 hour
Maps: 7½ ' Durango East

This is an easy hike out of Durango for those limited in time, but it gives a nice view down over the Fort Lewis College campus and part of Durango, and a good view of the east side of the La Platas and the south side of some of the San Juans.

"Raider Ridge" is a local name; there is no official name. This title comes from the name of the Fort Lewis College athletic teams; they are the "Raiders." At one time, the students maintained a big "R" on the campus side of this ridge; ecological outcries of some students and faculty have brought the policy of letting nature take its way again, and the "R" is growing faint.

Some of this ridge is private property; a big chunk is owned by Fort Lewis College and is open to the public. It is a steep sandstone uplift tilted ten to fifteen degrees to the southeast, known officially by geologists as a "hogback."

The Ridge can be ascended from the campus (northwest) side, but it is quite steep and very brushy this way. To hike up this side, go to the east end of Sixth Street. This curves around northeast uphill and at this point becomes Geoglein Gulch Road. As you round the corner, Burnett Construction Company will be immediately on your left. The next building beyond this, still on the left, will be the La Plata County Humane Society building. On the east side of the road here is a break in the bluff. You can begin climbing here; a little higher up are the remains of the "R," where there is less brush. This will take you to the top of the ridge.

The best and easiest route is from the southeast side off Horse Gulch Road. This is a four-wheel-drive road, very rocky at its beginning. To take this route, follow Eighth Avenue to Third Street, and go one block east to its end. Horse Gulch Road continues on at this point as a dirt road. If you have a two-wheel-drive vehicle, park at the end of Third Street and begin hiking here. With four-wheel-drive, follow Horse Gulch Road around northeast one mile, where you will find a turnout good enough for parking. Actually, you could drive to the top of the ridge, but then you wouldn't have a hike. So park at the turnout and begin hiking up the hill (west) up a little jeep road. Where the road forks, stay to the uphill side.

The hike is only one-half mile to the top, where the overlook views to the west are very nice.

If you would like to extend this hike, you can follow northeast along the ridge crest for a couple of miles. You can come back down the east side of the ridge most anywhere through the pinon-juniper forest to the road and hike back over the road to your vehicle.

Sometimes Durango has a mild winter, and this hike can be taken at that time of the year as well as at other seasons. The route from Horse Gulch presents the sunny side of the ridge, where snow tends to melt fairly rapidly. Usually deer and elk can be seen in this area during the winter, and deer year-round.

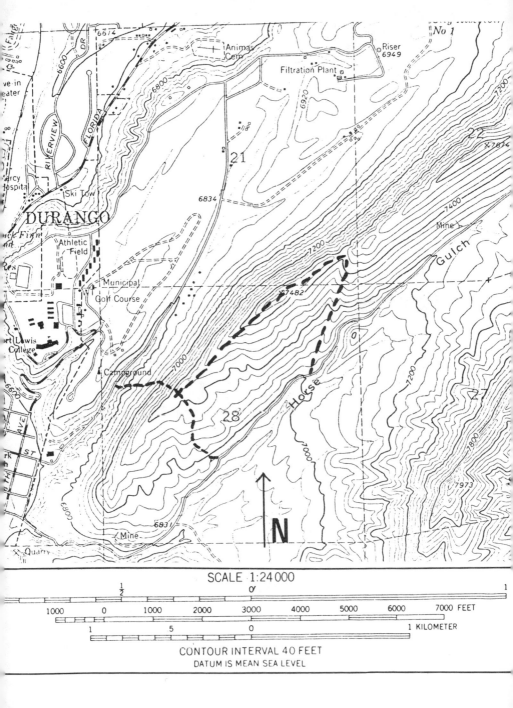

SCALE 1:24 000

1000 0 1000 2000 3000 4000 5000 6000 7000 FEET

1 5 0 1 KILOMETER

CONTOUR INTERVAL 40 FEET
DATUM IS MEAN SEA LEVEL

Twin Buttes.

Twin Buttes

Distance: 4 miles (round trip)
Starting Elevation: 6,630 feet
Elevation Gain: 1,107 feet
High Point: 7,737 feet
Rating: Easy, except last 300 feet, which are difficult
Time Allowed: 2½ to 3½ hours
Maps: 7½' Durango West

About two and one-fourth miles west of Durango and one-half mile north and above the highway off the southwest side of Perins Peak lies an interesting formation known as Twin Buttes. These buttes are paired close together; their tops are almost identical in height and are less than 200 yards straight-line distance apart. They are so symmetrical that they resemble identical twins and are thus properly named.

The approach can be made by two different routes, each with its own disadvantage, the one quite easy, the other less so. The easy route first. Its disadvantage is that it lies on private property and may not always be open to the public. For this approach, take U.S. Highway 160 out of Durango 1.3 miles west of the bridge over the Animas River to a little road that turns right 1 mile beyond the Four Winds Motel. It soon swings north into a low spot and then back around south and again west, where it starts to climb rather steeply. You should park at the bottom of this road for the hike; four-wheel-drive vehicles can make it all the way to the Buttes, but that would negate a pleasant and easy part of the hike. After climbing one-half mile, this road joins the old railroad right-of-way that used to bring coal down from the Boston Mine at Perins City. The route from here on is very gradual to the base of the Buttes, as it had to be to accommodate the train.

Once at the base of the Buttes, the climb is steep and a bit difficult, without benefit of trail. Several routes will work. North sides have much brush, so the southeast side of the first butte is a good route. The top is relatively flat and makes a good resting and viewing place.

To climb the second butte from the first, you can drop off the west side down a steep slope to the saddle between and up the east side of the second one. The descent is less than 200 feet, and the re-ascent is the same amount. An interesting start down from the east butte is offered on the southwest corner of the top, where cracks in the cap rock offer a nice little chimney to climb down through. This is not too high and just a right width to give you a little scrambling practice through a tight and relatively safe spot.

The second approach to the Buttes is from the northwest. For this route, take U.S. Highway 160 three and one-half miles out of Durango west to Lightner Creek Road. Turn right here and follow this road just over a mile north to where it makes a right-angle turn left downhill and crosses a little stream. Instead of making the turn, go straight ahead through a gate, and park just to the left of the road. This is state land. The disadvantage of this route is that it requires bushwhacking for the first one-half mile. The route is about .4 mile shorter than the other approach if you go the most efficient way.

From the parking spot, start climbing south just inside the fence; you can soon begin to angle more eastward. There is oak brush in the area, but most of it can be avoided by looking ahead. You should be able to see the buttes shortly after starting the climb. Aim uphill for a point half-way between the nearest butte and your starting point. This will bring you to a road on the old railroad right-of-way, which you can then follow easily in its winding way to the buttes. You can cross over behind the north side of the west butte and start climbing up the saddle between them. The northwest corner can be climbed, but the heavy brush there makes it unpleasant. The easiest way is to follow the road on around and start climbing up the saddle from the south side.

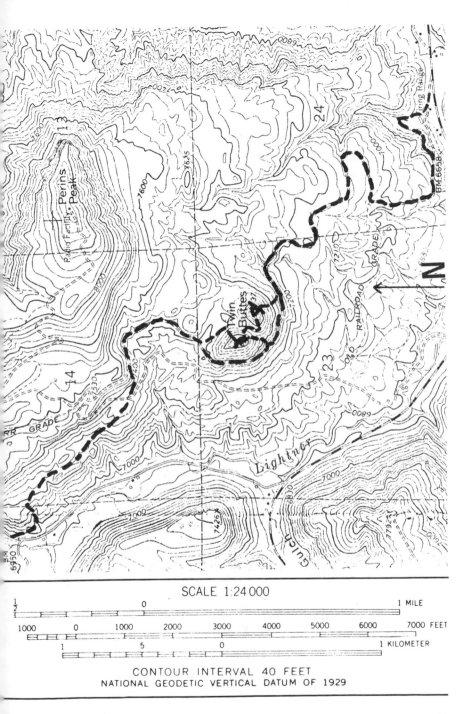

SCALE 1:24 000

1 MILE

1000   0   1000   2000   3000   4000   5000   6000   7000 FEET

1   5   0   1 KILOMETER

CONTOUR INTERVAL 40 FEET
NATIONAL GEODETIC VERTICAL DATUM OF 1929

Perins Peak

Distance: 5 miles (round trip)
Starting Elevation: 6,641 feet
Elevation Gain: 1,699 feet
High Point: 8,340 feet
Rating: Difficult
Time Allowed: 3 to 4 hours
Maps: 7½ ' Durango West
San Juan National Forest

Perins Peak is a critical area for an endangered species, the peregrine falcon; so you should avoid this hike during the most critical period, April 15 to August 30. Fortunately this is a period when higher climbs are beckoning the hiker.

This is a hike that can be taken directly from the city limits of Durango. Most of the mountain is owned by the Bureau of Land Management, with some of it owned by the Colorado State Division of Wildlife as winter feeding grounds for deer and elk. Big game is abundant here when the snow is deep in the high country. Sometimes this even includes the fall hunting season.

The first part is quite easy, but the last thousand feet of altitude gain are difficult due to steepness and slippery conditions. It is a good, vigorous hike and is rewarding for the exercise it provides and for the nice view of both the La Plata Mountains and Durango from the top. It is also a hike that can be taken even in the winter; I have done it on New Year's Day three times. This is possible because of good exposure to the sun at the higher levels.

To start, take Twenty-Second Street west off Main Street in Durango. In a couple of blocks, Twenty-Second turns south and climbs Crestview Mesa. At the top, it turns west again and becomes Montview Parkway. Follow it to Glenisle where you should turn left (south). At the end of Glenisle you come to Kearney. Park here and start hiking by climbing over the earth bank and across the stream (usually dry). At this point start climbing steeply uphill south and west through the thick oak brush. There are several twisting paths uphill through the brush; it is worth searching for one of these for the brush is formidable otherwise. Fortunately this steep brushy climb is only about a

Climbing the shale
rib of Perins Peak.

hundred feet high. At the top is a good open hiking and motorcycle trail; take it uphill (west) about a quarter mile. On the right
are the remains of an old jeep road. It is not obvious; so you will
need to move over to the north side of the hilltop you are on to
find it. Take this down to the valley below where you should find
a trail going west toward the Peak. Follow this along the small
stream (which it crosses several times) northwesterly. At about
one-half mile upstream, the trail leaves the stream and climbs a
steep ridge of gray Mancos shale. This point is not marked, but it
is crucial to find, since farther on you will have to climb out
through brush and steep hillsides. Because some people do hike
on upstream a ways, a trail is visible here. The turnoff can be
recognized thus: there is a little flat place on the west side of the
stream where the stream makes a turn east and then sharply back
west. The shale ridge rises out of this flat place. If you look up it
(west), you should be able to see the trail. The trail rises sharply
at first and contours around this ridge in a general westerly
direction toward the face of Perins Peak. Perins itself has a distinctive profile. Its top has a sharp, pointed cliff that faces east

and looks down over Durango like a guardian.

One-half mile along the ridge brings you to a trail division where one branch turns left and leads south up Hogsback Ridge. Your trail goes on west toward the face of Perins. On your left will be a steep shale hillside leading down into Evergreen Valley; on your right will be a tangle of brush. At one point, you have to traverse a bit of the steep shale; there is usually a narrow path (six to ten inches wide) along this area. Sometimes bits of the path have slipped away, and you simply have to dig in your boots for a foothold. Fortunately, the shale is usually soft. Just beyond this, you swing northwest and ascend toward a large shale rib coming down from the peak. There is a well-defined path in this area on up the rib. There are several of these ribs. The correct one ascends to a point just to the left of the pointed cliff. If you are on the correct rib, you will come to one last lonely pinon tree hanging on to life in the shale. At thirty to forty yards above the tree, you leave the path and start making your own way; there is no more significant path the rest of the way, though you may strike some game trails that are useful for a ways.

At the turnoff point above the tree, go left and traverse the steep sides of a shale gulley. Into the gulley and out the far side is less than fifty yards, but it is the most hazardous part of the hike, for a loosened footstep could give you a long ride to the bottom of the shale. Fortunately, some brush is available for grasping along the climb out, where it is steepest.

Once over the far edge of the gulley, you will find yourself in a mixture of rocks and some brush. This is a slow area but not dangerous. Pick your way along a contour toward the base of the cliff at its southeast corner. This appears to be a cliff of mud and shale with some ominous cracks in it. I like to stay a little below this. Once beyond the cliff, going southwest, you can turn back north for the final assault. You will have about 500 feet of steep ascent over big rocks and through some brush. Stay west of the cliffs some fifty feet or more for safety's sake and for more openness in the brush.

At the top of the rocks is a sandstone wall ten to thirty feet straight up. I have a favorite old dead tree that I can climb easily in three well-placed steps to a low bench on this wall. Once over this, it is an easy 100 yards through oak brush to the top. If you miss my tree, you can contour further west around the base of the wall to a usable break in it. Now you are above the pointed cliff face and are ready to collect your reward for the effort you have

On Perins Peak after crossing the hazardous gully.

expended. Go east from your top-out point to the rocky point. But exercise care as you go out there, remembering how far up you are.

The actual highest point is an easy quarter mile west of the face cliff. Since it is bare, you can get fine views in all directions. Also, you will find near the top two objects that look like large blank billboards. They are microwave reflectors.

The mileage and time listed in the heading presuppose a return over the approach route. But there are a couple of other options, one north and one west. Either one will leave you some distance from your starting point. The north route will leave you a two-mile hike back through town if you have not left a car there. The west route will leave you about six miles out of town. Both are interesting routes and worth the trouble of putting another car at the terminal point.

I will describe both routes, the north one first. They start out alike. There is an old four-wheel-drive road, now abandoned, that reaches the top of the peak from the west. Follow this down one-half mile to where it just begins to level out. For the north route, turn right at this point down the head of the first drainage that you reach from the top of the peak. This is an open meadow area. There is a trail, but the beginning of it tends to be grassed over. Hike down this trail and turn right at the edge of the trees.

This should put you on the remains of an old road that zigzags down a canyon northeasterly. This route is not as steep as the one leading up the mountain. This trail is well defined down through the canyon and tall timber. The price of an easier trail is a longer distance. From the top back to the edge of town by this route is four miles versus the two and one-half miles on the climb route.

At the end of the canyon, the trail disappears in a grassy meadow area. Just keep moving northeasterly, as you did in the canyon. In about a quarter mile, you should cross a stream and find an old road on the other side. If you keep upstream a bit, you will only be called upon to cross a little marshy area. Downstream a bit you will face an arroyo that is eight feet deep.

Once on the road, follow it east (right) into town, where you should come out at or near the head of Clovis Drive.

For the westerly route, come down from the top the same way. A little beyond the north route turnoff, the road divides in a flat area. Take the left fork here downhill. You will need to watch closely for the beginning of this left fork since it has recently been bulldozed full of brush and dirt.

An interesting feature of this route is the site of Perins City and the Boston Coal Mine. About a quarter mile down from the road divide, you come to another level spot. Go to the northwest end to find the site of the town and the mine.

No buildings remain here, but the place was once very busy, being one of the largest coal mines in southwest Colorado. It was active during the first quarter of the twentieth century. A railroad wound its way up the mountainside to carry out the coal.

You could hike out the old right-of-way, but it is very long due to the gradual grade that the train could tolerate. The recommended route down from here is to go west and a little south over the side of this mountain. This will be bushwhacking through some oak brush, but you can go around most of it. There are 600 feet more of descent. Many summer lupines bloom profusely on this hillside. You will have to cross a fence or two, but the land is public on both sides—some of it U.S. land and some belongs to the state. You should end up on Dry Creek Road just to the north of Lightner Creek Road, one and one-fourth miles north of U.S. Highway 160.

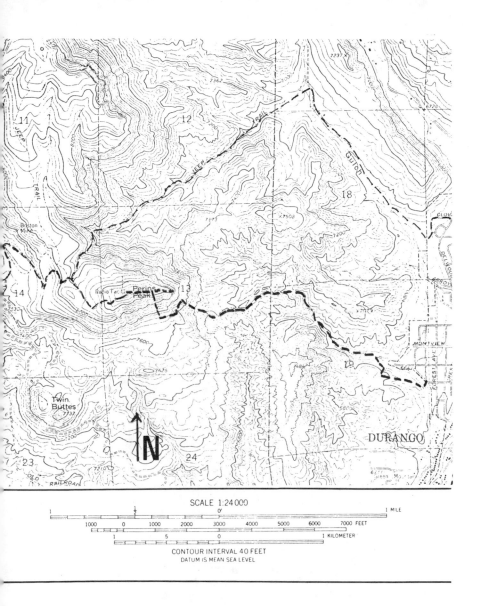

SCALE 1:24 000

CONTOUR INTERVAL 40 FEET
DATUM IS MEAN SEA LEVEL

Haflin Creek half way up.

CHAPTER 3

Hikes Up and On Missionary Ridge

Haflin Creek

Distance: 3.2 miles (one way)
Starting Elevation: 6,620 feet
Elevation Gain: 2,780 feet
High Point: 9,400 feet
Rating: Moderate
Time Allowed: 3 hours
Maps: 7½' Durango East
San Juan National Forest

For those who like to hike in deep woods, Haflin Canyon makes a good half-day hike. It takes you up from the Animas Valley through nearly 3,000 feet of ascent, almost always among trees. This hike also illustrates very well the different climatic zones and the associated forestation. At the bottom, you start among pinon, junipers, and oak brush. Soon you reach a level of Ponderosa pine; this gives way to quaking aspen and the beginning of spruce and fir.

Haflin is a small creek in a deep and rugged canyon that

breaks through the west, steep side of Missionary Ridge. You start near the creek, rise high above it, later come even with it, and cross it, and finally rise through an open brushy area to the top of the ridge above the stream source. In this brushy area, you can get good views to the west of the river valley from which you have come and to the La Platas beyond.

To take this trail, leave Durango east on Thirty-Second Street off Main Street about 1.2 miles to a left turn on East Animas Road. At just over five miles up this road, you should see a sign (on the east side of the road) for Haflin Creek Trail. Off-the-road parking is available here.

The trail starts off nearly flat in an easterly direction but soon launches into a series of climbing switchbacks, some of them a bit steep. The first one is a bit obscure; it switches sharply to the left and up a few yards before reaching a little white building that sits at the mouth of the canyon. The trail eventually parallels the stream that is cascading and falling far below. The trail is easy to follow most of the way until the stream rises up to it where there is some old flooding debris in a fairly flat area. This is the one place where the trail is sometimes not quite clear, but at the upper end of this flat area, it begins to rise up the hillside again out the north side after crossing and recrossing the creek. Not far above this you come out into a steep, brushy area and, in a series of switchbacks, arrive at the top of the ridge where this trail joins the Missionary Ridge Trail in the aspen.

This is listed as a half-day hike, but you could lengthen it by going either north or south on the Missionary Ridge Trail. This is why distance and time for this hike are listed as one way. Returning on Haflin Creek Trail would complete a half day.

South on the Missionary Ridge Trail, hiking is good for a couple of miles, but beyond that the trail soon descends to private property, causing an access problem.

North on this trail soon brings you to the top of Baldy Mountain (9,805 feet). Beyond this point lie several possible descent routes. Within five and one-half miles are three easterly descents and one westerly descent. The westerly descent is Stevens Creek. It is shown on the national forest map but is not recommended because much of the trail is inadequately maintained, and even if you find the beginning of it, you are most likely to lose the trail later. The easterly descents are in order with mileages from Baldy: First Fork (1.5 miles), Red Creek (2.6 miles), Shearer Creek (5.5 miles). These all lead down to Florida Road or other roads leading to Florida Road. All these trails will be discussed separately.

No part of this hike is difficult, but it is rated moderate because of the relatively large amount of altitude gain. It is well worth the effort because of the variations of trees, the wild flowers, and the changing vistas.

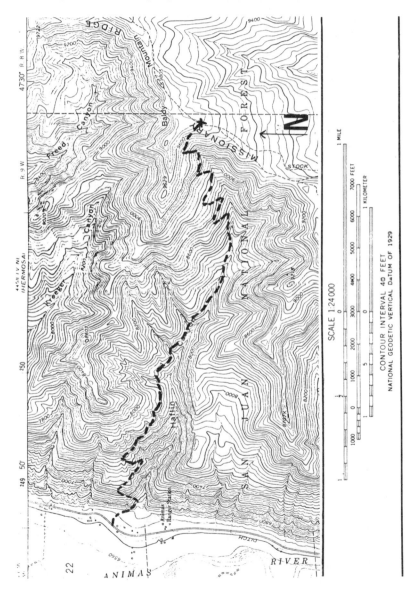

Wallace Lake

Distance: 1 mile (round trip)
Starting Elevation: 8,200 feet
Elevation Gain: 200 feet
High Point: 8,400 feet
Rating: Easy
Time Allowed: 1 hour
Maps: 7½' Hermosa
San Juan National Forest

This is a very easy hike in a nice, secluded area (except during hunting season). It is located well up on the west side of Missionary Ridge and is surrounded by big trees, mostly aspen. The hike itself is short, but the hiking area is several miles from Durango. Still, it is a pleasant drive.

The trail is reached via the East Animas and Missionary Ridge roads. From Durango, take Thirty-Second Street east off the north end of Main Street. Thirty-Second runs into and stops at East Animas Road. Turn left on it (north), and follow it nine and one-half miles to where Missionary Ridge Road branches off to the right, uphill. People approaching from the north can turn off U.S. Highway 550 at Baker's Bridge Road. Follow this road across the Animas River and south to Missionary Ridge Road, which will be a sharp left turn back and uphill.

Missionary Ridge Road is gravel and often plagued by a washboard effect. It also climbs steeply up a series of many switchbacks. So it is a slow road, but it yields fine views of the Animas Valley from a higher and higher perspective. Westward across the valley, the Hermosa Cliffs and La Plata Mountains grow ever more impressive as you continue to climb.

After climbing Missionary Ridge Road for a little less than six miles, you come to the Wallace Lake turnoff. There should be ample parking here. Actually, four-wheel-drive vehicles can go on to the lake, but the hike is pleasant and short. Shortly after the trail begins, the road branches. Go to the right, and you will soon be at the lake. Actually, there are two other small lakes. You reach the main lake first, with the others to the right and left of it. All of these lakes are shallow. In dry years, they sometimes dry up completely. Whether there is water or not, it is a peaceful and lovely spot. During the fall, it is surrounded by golden-clad aspen.

Those who want a more vigorous hike can follow the jeep road on around to the right alongside two of the lakes. It twists and turns and climbs another three and one-half miles up to 9,500 feet. It passes through big timber and a couple of open spots. At the 9,500 foot spot, you will be on a ridge dividing the Stevens Creek and Wallace Lake drainages. The short route back to Wallace is one mile northwest, but you must bushwhack down the steep side of the basin, following the creek to the uppermost of the three lakes.

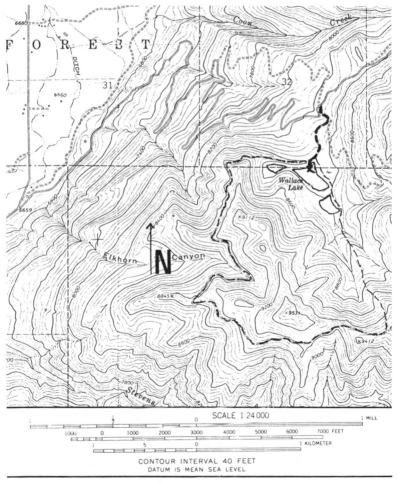

SCALE 1:24000

CONTOUR INTERVAL 40 FEET
DATUM IS MEAN SEA LEVEL

45

Mountain View Crest

Distance: 9 to 10 miles (round trip)
Starting Elevation: 11,480 feet (10,600 feet)
Elevation Gain: 1,518 feet (2,398 feet)
High Point: 12,998 feet
Rating: Moderate (long and high but not difficult)
Time Allowed: 7 to 8 hours
Maps: 7½ ' Mountain View Crest
San Juan National Forest

This hike lies northeast of Durango over a number of miles of gravel road (usually somewhat rough) and a short distance of four-wheel-drive road. So access is slow, but the end of the trail offers some of the most fantastic scenery in Colorado. I am going to suggest some variations on the terminal area that will vary time, mileage, and altitude. The statistics given above are about medium for the options. Once in the area, you will want to take advantage of the full range of views. I have made this hike in a half day, but a long, full day is much better to allow you to get a good exposure to its riches.

To find this area, go to Thirty-Second Street off the north end of Main Street in Durango. Follow Thirty-Second east to its end (1.2 miles) at East Animas Road. Follow this road north 9.5 miles to where Missionary Ridge Road separates off uphill to the right. This is a climbing gravel road with many switchbacks. Follow it nineteen miles to where Henderson Lake Road branches off to the right. This is a four-wheel-drive road about four miles long, but two-wheel-drive vehicles can make half or more of it when the road is dry. The road ends at the wilderness barrier, where you will find plenty of parking space. At this point, hike straight north along the east side of Lime Mesa, following the old jeep road past Dollar Lake to a saddle at the east end of Mountain View Crest.

Those who must stop farther back with two-wheel-drive cars will have to hike an extra mile or more and gain an extra 800 feet. They need not hike all the way to the wilderness barrier. Where the road goes northeast and turns sharply back south, climbing, hikers should head straight north along the west side of the Lime Mesa. In 1.3 miles you come to the north end of it; the trail is pretty good along most of this route. At the north end of the mesa you are at timberline; swing right here across the tundra. A quarter mile beyond, you should intersect the old jeep road described above. Take it left another one and one-half miles to the saddle at the east end of Mountain View Crest.

Lunch stop on the way to Mountain View Crest, Lime Mesa on the left, Dollar Lake just ahead.

At the saddle you begin to see the dramatic views, but they are even better if you climb left a quarter mile to the top of the first rise (12,802 feet). The second rise, a quarter mile beyond, is called Overlook Point, and it stands at 12,998 feet.

The drama is below and beyond—in the form of four beautiful lakes. To the right and below Overlook Point lies, first, Ruby Lake, and a little further north and lower, Emerald Lake. To the left and down are Pear Lake and Webb Lake. All of these provide excellent trout fishing. To go down to them commits you to an overnight stay, for they are further away than they first appear. Overlook Point is the only place from which all four lakes can be seen. The first top only reveals Ruby and Emerald.

But the view down to the lakes is only the start of the scenery. Far below them is Needle Creek—too far down to see—but across Needle Canyon and abruptly above rise Pidgeon and Turret peaks. Pidgeon is higher at 13,972 feet and drops a sheer 1,000 feet on its east side to the saddle between it and Turret, which rises up the other side to 13,835 feet. These two miss being fourteeners by a small margin, but there is no more dramatic view in the San Juan Mountains. Viewing the east face of Pidgeon can send shivers up and down your back, let alone standing on its top.

There is still more to see, if you have time.

Go back to the original saddle overlooking Ruby Lake. From this point, pick up a trail going east, and hike three miles. You can end up climbing north off the trail to the top of Mount Kennedy. It has a double top, with the farthest being the highest (13,125 feet). Either top will give about the same view.

The view here is to the north into Chicago Basin, surrounded by the Needles—three fourteeners. They are, from west to east, Eolus, Sunlight, and Windom. This is one of the most popular backpacking areas in the state. People ride the Durango-Silverton train to Needleton and hike nine miles up Needle Creek to Chicago Basin, where a base camp can be established for climbing all three peaks.

While the three fourteeners, in my opinion, are not quite as dramatic as Pidgeon, they are certainly powerful and majestic. This is truly wilderness area par excellence. Behind them you get glimpses of the tops of other peaks showing through the saddles.

By this time, you should know that I have described more than the mileage given in the heading. It would be a very long hike to cover all of this and get back to your car in one day, so you may have to make a choice whether you do the east or west side from the saddle. In any case, the return to the starting point will repeat the approach route.

Pigeon and Turret Peaks across Needle Creek Valley from Mountain View Crest.

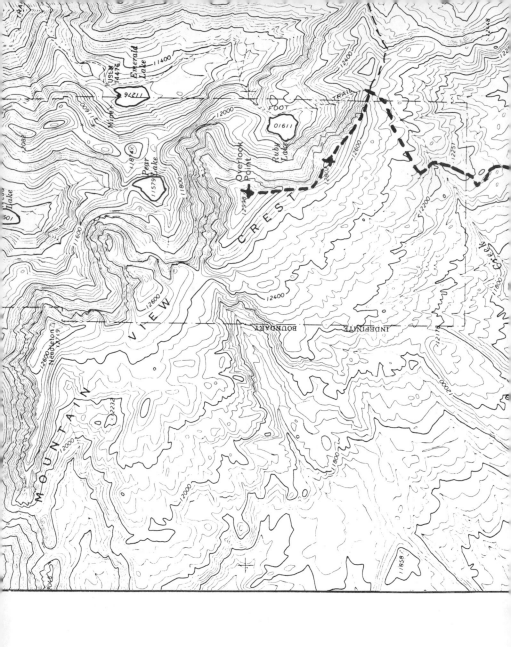

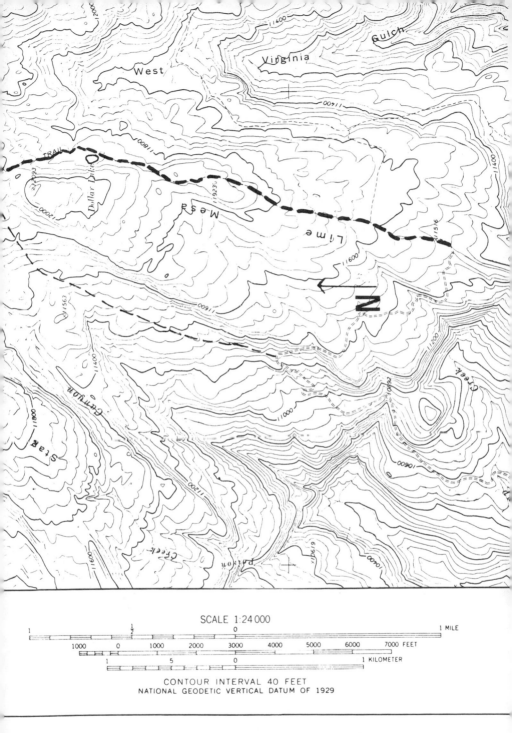

SCALE 1:24000

1   ½   0   1 MILE

1000   0   1000   2000   3000   4000   5000   6000   7000 FEET

1   5   0   1 KILOMETER

CONTOUR INTERVAL 40 FEET
NATIONAL GEODETIC VERTICAL DATUM OF 1929

Burnt Timber Trail

Distance: 6.5 miles (round trip)
Starting Elevation: 8,500 feet
Elevation Gain: 2,500 feet
High Point: 11,000 feet
Rating: Easy
Time Allowed: 2½ to 3½ hours
Maps: 7½' Lemon Reservoir
7½' Needle Mountains
San Juan National Forest

Some hikers may think that the easy rating for this trail is underrated because of the climbing, but there is nothing difficult about any part of it. It just goes steadily upward at a good incline and requires a slower pace and more rest for some hikers than other easy trails.

This is a rewarding hike, for it traverses genuine backcountry and stays near the rugged Florida River canyon. The east side of this canyon presents a high, imposing wall of timber and rock. Most of this hike is in the trees along the base of the east side of Missionary Ridge, but there are frequent views eastward through the trees. The last mile shuts off the eastward view while passing through a high-altitude open, but steep, meadow.

To find the trail head from Durango, take East Third Avenue north to its end, and turn right (northeast) on Florida Road. Follow this out of town thirteen miles to Lemon Lake Road. This spot is easily recognized: the main road here turns right at a ninety-degree angle around a little country store and crosses Florida River. Lemon Lake Road goes straight on at the turn and is gravel. A couple of miles up this road you come to the dam, behind which is impounded beautiful Lemon Lake or, more properly, Lemon Reservoir. This is an irrigation supply filled by melting winter snows. It is peaceful and inviting, nestled as it is at the base of high wooded hills on each side. Lemon is a favorite fishing and picnicking spot with several good sites along its banks.

To reach the trail, drive along the side of the lake and two miles beyond its north end. Here you cross a cattle guard; one road goes straight on up Miller Mountain, but you should turn left into the Florida Campground. In a quarter mile you cross Florida River, then immediately turn left. There are two left options here; the sharpest left is only a camping loop. Take the other one. It winds on around south, west, and north again for a mile and ends up in Transfer Park Campground, tucked into a flat spot next to the river. This is an excellent and secluded camping spot.

Plenty of parking space is available where you first enter the campground, at the northwest corner. The trail begins at the north side of this area.

The trail is a good one—it is well maintained and easy to follow. It is used by horseback riders as well as hikers. The three and one-fourth miles (one way) given in the heading takes you to the old Burnt Timber Road along the top of Missionary Ridge. Some may wish to turn back shortly after entering the meadow instead of climbing on up to the road, which is a mile further and 800 feet higher; you would then have to follow the trail still further to get good views of surrounding peaks. Others may want to go even further, for the trail continues, eventually coming to a crossover to Lime Mesa Trail west and north or going on to a turn eastward that takes you to Durango City Reservoir, some thirteen miles from Transfer Park. This is beautiful country but carries you into backpacking instead of day hiking distances.

The projected six and one-half mile hike presupposes returning to Transfer Park from Burnt Timber Road by the same route as you came.

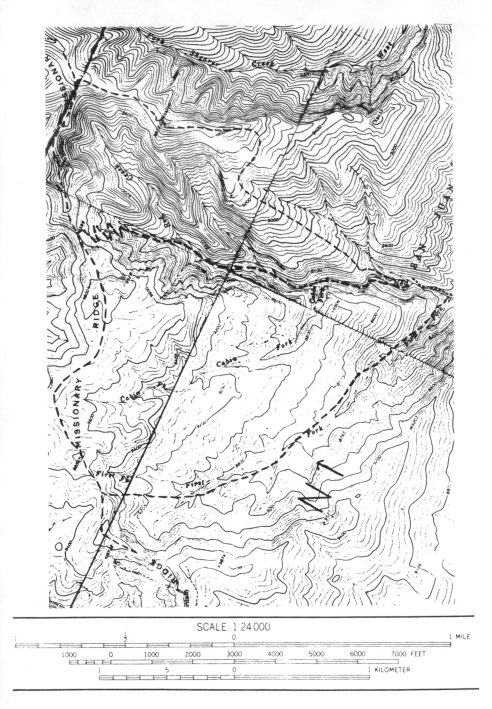

SCALE 1 24 000

1 MILE

1000   0   1000   2000   3000   4000   5000   6000   7000 FEET

1   5   0   1 KILOMETER

Red Creek Trail

Distance: 6 miles (round trip)
Starting Elevation: 8,080 feet
Elevation Gain: 1,519 feet
High Point: 9,599 feet
Rating: Easy
Time Allowed: 2½ to 3½ hours
Maps: 7½' Rules Hill
    7½' Lemon Reservoir } *The trail goes through*
    7½' Hermosa   *the corners of these*
    7½' Durango East   *four maps.*
    San Juan National Forest

      Red Creek Trail is a lovely hike anytime the snow is not too deep, but it is especially good on a warm summer day, for most of the way it follows a nice gurgling stream at the bottom of a narrow canyon in the shade of big fir, spruce, and aspen trees. The trail is well maintained and easy to follow. It climbs quite gradually for two and one-half miles, then, steeply, up a series of switchbacks the last half mile to the top of Missionary Ridge.

      To get to Red Creek from Durango, take East Third Avenue north to its end and turn right on Florida Road. Follow this road northeast out of town ten miles to a left turn uphill (north), where there should be a sign reading "Colvig Silver Camps—1 mile." this is a good gravel road for that distance. At the Camps, you get the impression that the road is about to end, but it does not; continue north, right through the Camps for another mile. This second mile is much narrower and rougher. At the end of the second mile, turn left off the road across the stream. There is currently a sign marked "Red Creek Trail" at the turn off. Just across the stream there is a shaded open spot for parking. The trail begins at the west side of this open area.

      The quality of the approach road varies. Recently it has been fairly good, but sometimes it is washed out to the point that only four-wheel-drive vehicles can make it all the way to this area. When it is in that condition two-wheel drives will need to park 300 yards short of the turn off at the bottom of the last hill, which is often washed out and full of big rocks. Anyway, it adds only a short distance to the total hike to have to walk up the hill.

The hike itself, after leaving the road, stays close to the creek, crossing it occasionally, as it gradually rises through the timber. Because the last half mile to the top is much steeper, those who want a very easy hike could turn around at this point. The steep part, however, is really not too bad; it is used by horses. In fact this is a favorite trail for the elk hunters in the fall.

Red Creek Trail terminates in a saddle at the top of the ridge, where it runs into Missionary Ridge Trail. This is a very good trail where Red Creek joins it. For hikers who want to go further, this trail can be hiked northeast or southwest for some distance. The San Juan National Forest map shows it going south all the way to Florida Road two miles east of Durango. However, the last two miles or more of the trail are not usable, for they pass through private property that is restricted by locked gates and "No Trespassing" signs.

The distance figure of six miles given in the trail description at the beginning assumes turning around at the union with the Missionary Ridge Trail. However, this hike can be extended into a good loop hike that brings you back to the starting point by a different route. To take the loop go northeast along Missionary Ridge. The trail begins to climb gradually right away and in a short distance shifts to a steep climb of 350 feet. At the top of this it levels off in a grove of big trees. In a short distance (a few hundred yards) a good trail (currently unmarked) swings off the main trail to the right (southeast); take this for the return. It starts out level but begins shortly to descend gradually.

Once on the right trail, it is fairly easy to follow, though the last time I was over it there was some need of maintenance due to aspen logs that had fallen across it.

The trail follows a very narrow ridge between the main branch of Red Creek and West Fork of Shearer Creek for over a mile. While this ridge is well timbered, it is a delightful hiking area due to the fine views down each side, especially the Shearer Creek (east) side. You can look down a canyon wall of some 600 feet and across a heavily wooded area for several miles beyond. The last time I was there in the early fall I heard a bull elk bugling in the distance below.

Where the narrow ridge begins to broaden, the trail remains high and close to the Shearer Canyon overlook for another half mile or more before starting more steeply downhill to the southwest. In less than another half mile, the trail joins an old logging road and descends in a series of switchbacks for more than another mile to a usable jeep road. A few hundred yards down this road and you should come to the recommended parking place. Just before the last descent the road splits; if you should happen to take the left side and miss the last ridge never fear for that side will take you down a steep incline to a small stream; across it, the road turns right and in a short distance also comes back to where you crossed the stream to park. The loop route is less than a mile longer than the round trip over Red Creek both ways.

This loop hike could also be done in reverse, but there is more difficulty following it, for the logging road after you have climbed it a ways, splits several times. If you do miss the right one, continue uphill northeast to the Shearer Canyon rim and follow the previous directions in reverse. Somewhere along this rim you should be able to find the trail.

Another longer loop trip can be taken using the First Fork trail to climb to Missionary Ridge and then returning via Red Creek Trail. It is about 10 miles long, a good day hike. This trail begins a quarter mile earlier than the Red Creek Trail. It currently has a sign marking its starting point. Coming up the same approach road you turn left before climbing the last hill on the road and begin the trail on the north (uphill) side of a small fenced-in corral. The trail moves west near the stream for more than two miles before emerging into an open meadow that gradually slopes uphill toward the ridge. The trail tends to be hard to track in the meadow, but you should be able to pick it up again by moving uphill to the right at about forty-five degrees from the approach. This will be northerly. There is a cliff to be bypassed. If you do not find the trail you can head anywhere toward the top of the ridge after getting around the cliff. This part is heavily wooded. At the top, turn right on Missionary Ridge Trail through woods and charming meadows and across some easy rises. In about two miles you descend into the small saddle where the Red Creek Trail begins its steep descent down the switchbacks referred to earlier. In three miles this brings you back to the road. A quarter mile down that you will get back to the First Fork Trail beginning. This loop could also be done in reverse, but at the top of the ridge it is harder to find the beginning of the descent down First Fork Trail.

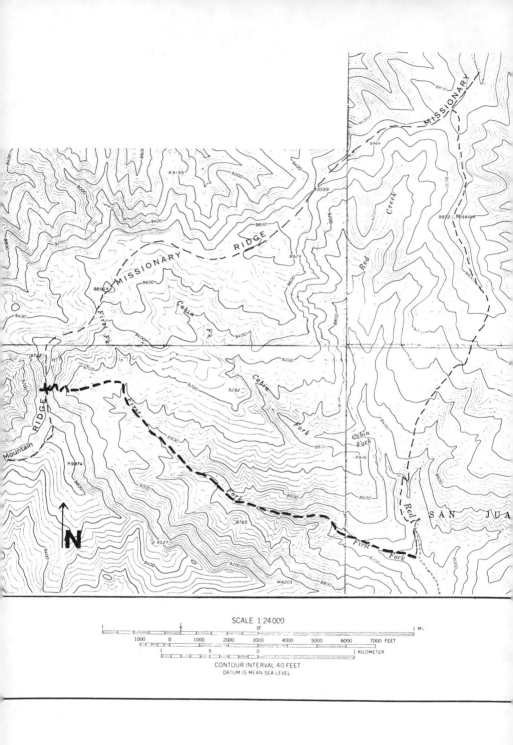

SCALE 1:24 000

CONTOUR INTERVAL 40 FEET
DATUM IS MEAN SEA LEVEL

Shearer Creek

Distance: 11 miles (round trip)
Starting Elevation: 7,560 feet
Elevation Gain: 2,640 feet
High Point: 10,200 feet
Rating: Easy, but fairly long
Time Allowed: 4½ to 6 hours
Maps:7½ ' Rules Hill
       7½ ' Lemon Reservoir
      San Juan National Forest

This is a delightful hike to the top of Missionary Ridge from a southeasterly approach. It starts out climbing a hill above Florida Road and in one mile joins Shearer Creek, which it follows closely almost all the way to the top. The rise is quite gradual most of the way except at the top.

To take the hike from Durango, go east from Main Street downtown on any street to East Third Avenue; follow it north to its end, and turn right at Florida Road. Follow it northeast out of town twelve miles to the beginning of the trail. On the right is the parking lot of the Cowboy Restaurant, which is itself hidden in big trees near Florida River. Across the road on the west side is a small turnout and parking area. Just above this you should see a large national forest sign announcing "Shearer Creek Trail." Park here, and begin the hike uphill through a wooden gate. The first two miles are through private property, so you must stay on the trail. However, the forest service has legal access for the public through this area. The trail is well marked and is fairly easy to follow uphill through large Ponderosa pines.

In one mile, the trail joins the creek and follows it most of the way to the top of Missionary Ridge. The trail crosses and re-crosses the stream many times. It is a gurgling, pleasant little stream in the summer and fall and is easily crossed on the rocks. To hike at the bottom of a deep canyon among big trees is an enjoyable way to spend a few hours.

In the spring and early summer during the snowmelt, the stream is higher and much harder to cross, so this trail is not recommended until the major snowpack is gone at levels of 10,000 feet and lower.

The trail joins a road at the top of Missionary Ridge on a side ridge that reaches southeast fairly level for two miles. The point of this side ridge overlooks Lemon Lake 2,000 feet below, but it is heavily wooded, making it hard to see the lake.

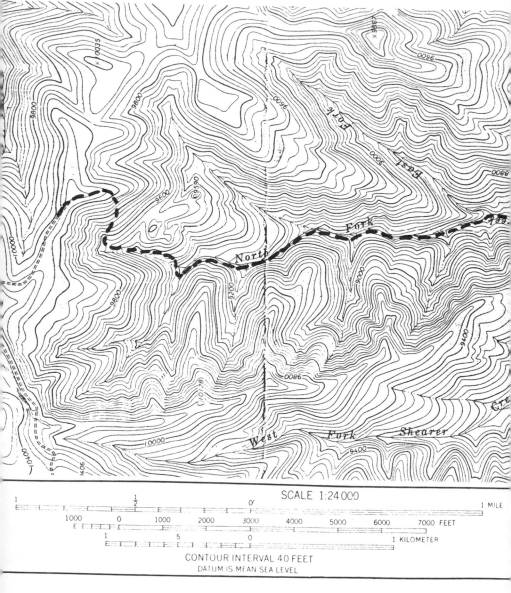

SCALE 1:24 000

CONTOUR INTERVAL 40 FEET
DATUM IS MEAN SEA LEVEL

The return is by the same route as the climb. There is one problem on the return—in the last mile after you leave the stream, there are enough cow paths to obscure the main trail. However, a southeasterly route through here will still get you down to Florida Road even if a little off the correct route.

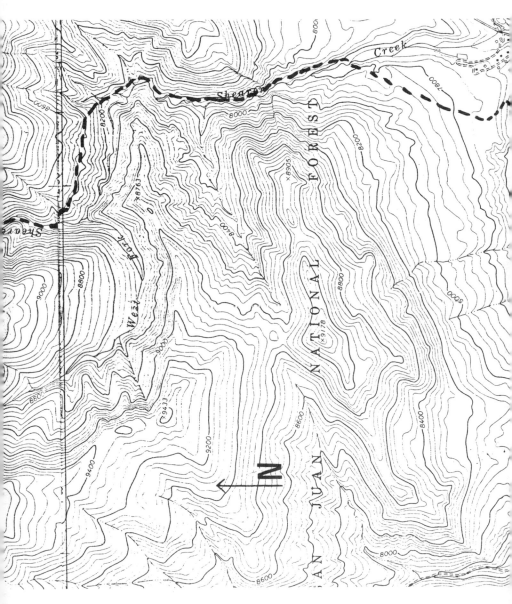

Looking down the west ridge below Mount Baker toward La Plata Canyon and across to the western La Plata mountains

CHAPTER 4

La Plata
Mountain Climbs

Kennebec Pass—Taylor Lake

Distance: 3 miles (round trip)
Starting Elevation: 10,240 feet
Elevation Gain: 1,520 feet
High Point: 11,760 feet
Rating: Moderate
Time Allowed: 2 hours
Maps: 7½' Monument Hill
 7½' La Plata
 San Juan National Forest

This is a relatively short hike following a long drive on a gravel road, but both the drive and the hike are well worth it. The drive starts at 7,000 feet and slowly winds its way up to the trail head at 10,240 feet, nearly two-thirds of a mile of altitude gain. It rises through pinon-juniper country, up through Ponderosa. Eventually, tall aspen close in on and near the road, along with spruce and fir. During the first ten miles, there are several breaks in the forest that give receding vistas of Durango down in the valley. At about twelve to fifteen miles you come to Rand's Point, where there is a turnout on the left side of the road. Stopping here is well worthwhile, for you look far down into Junction Creek Canyon and across its headwaters to the steep sides of Cumberland Mountain, Snowstorm Peak, and Lewis Mountain. These are among the highest peaks of the east range of the La Platas. Kennebec Pass, the hiking objective, is also visible between Cumberland and a high flat ridge north of it.

To reach the trail head, take Main Street in Durango to a west turn on Twenty-Fifth Street. In a couple of blocks, this curves off to the northwest and becomes Junction Street. Take this out of town, where it becomes Junction Creek Road. The road follows Junction Creek all the way to the national forest boundary. The forest boundary is easily recognized, for the blacktop stops here with a cattle guard.

At the cattle guard, check your speedometer. Driving on a gravel road from here on will be slow due to many curves, a steady uphill climb, and often a washboard effect in the surface. (This is great deer and elk country; your chances of seeing deer are quite good; elk occasionally appear, but they are more apt to stay further away from the road.) Drive up this road seventeen and one-half miles (allow for some variation of speedometers). At this point you come to a road that turns left. A very large post will be on either side of the road about twenty yards in from Junction Creek Road. On the right post there should be a sign pointing to "Sharkstooth Trail." Follow this road (south) eight-tenths mile to the trail head. Here, a wide spot a few yards north of the trail head provides suitable parking space.

When I hiked this trail in mid-August, the wild flowers were abundant; open places displayed great patches of blue, larkspur, and alpine asters, punctuated with yellow daisies. Further up were many other kinds of wild flowers. When I hiked this trail in early October, the aspen trees were aflame with gold.

As you near the pass, the trail traverses an open rocky area that yields a view southeastward down the entire Junction Creek Canyon to Durango. The canyon is heavily wooded in dark green; a glance upward toward the pass and Cumberland Mountain shows the light green of tundra above timberline. Every view from this trail is different and beautiful. A quarter mile further brings you to the pass. Here the views north and northeast give the best skyline panorama in southwest Colorado. You see the

Needles, Twilight and the West Needles, the Grenadiers, Sultan, Engineer, Grizzly, and many others. If you hike 150 yards down the other side of the pass, you see around the west side of the ridge on the north side of the pass, and more of the panorama opens up: Lizzard Head, the Wilsons, Dolores Peak, and Lone Cone.

If you are interested in mining history, you can hike a quarter mile southeast from the pass to an old mine that is in a better stage of preservation than some. It is in an exposed area above timberline, so the views are excellent.

The three miles specified in the heading are based on a return from Kennebec to the starting point. This is a fairly easy hike, though a bit steep.

Taylor Lake can also be included in this hike. It adds another 1.8 miles (one way) to the distance. There is a four-wheel-drive road up to Kennebec from the west. To go to Taylor, take this road down the west side of the pass and a half mile to where the road turns left and down the hill to Cumberland Basin; at this turn, the trail goes on west to the lake. From the pass to the lake is easy hiking with not much altitude change. There are usually many wild flowers in abundance along this route. Also, if time permits, a side trip down into Cumberland Basin (one-half mile) will be rewarded by even more wild flowers and another mining area.

The trail does go on southwest from Taylor Lake, where it climbs a ridge, drops down into Bear Creek Canyon, and goes up the other side to the pass between Sharkstooth and Centennial Peak. This is described as a separate hike, approached from the west—a much shorter and easier route for that area.

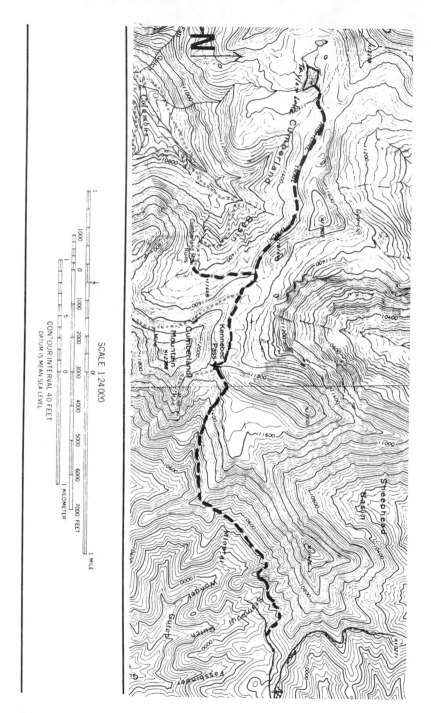

SCALE 1:24 000

CONTOUR INTERVAL 40 FEET
DATUM IS MEAN SEA LEVEL

Silver Mountain

Distance: 5.3 miles (round trip)
Starting Elevation: 9,400 feet
Elevation Gain: 3,050 feet
High Point: 12,450 feet
Rating: Difficult
Time Allowed: 5 to 6 hours
Maps: 7½' La Plata
San Juan National Forest

Silver Mountain is a vigorous climb on the east ridge of the La Plata Mountains. It is the highest point at the south end of this ridge. Strong parties can do it in a long half day, perhaps beating the time given above. The first half of the ascent is easy, but the upper half gets quite steep in places. All of the La Plata climbs are rewarded with fine views from the top. The view from Silver is the best from the southeast corner.

The hike starts out of La Plata Canyon. The road is located ten and one-half miles west of Durango off U.S. Highway 160. The canyon road turns north one quarter mile west of the Hesperus Post Office. This road is blacktop the first four miles—to Mayday. Beyond this point it is gravel; follow it another five miles. It gets a bit rough, but two-wheel drives can usually make it all right. The stopping point has room for four cars. There should be a sign recommending four-wheel drives only beyond this point. Some old mine buildings are located here. A little road drops down to the right and terminates in a good picnic spot a hundred yards down, beside the La Plata River. You may park at the top or bottom of this little road.

The hike starts with its first hazard—crossing the river. Since this area has a good deal of foot traffic, there is usually a pretty good log to cross over. Just over the river two or three hundred yards you come to the ruins of the Gold King Mill. It was one of the largest ever to operate in the canyon. It can be seen easily from the west side of the river and is another sign that you are at the right place. It is still impressive even in its state of decay. Much of the roof structure remains intact. It was a large stamping operation that continued well into the twentieth century.

Silver Mountain. Mount Baker is on the left ridge; Deadwood Mountain and its descending ridge are on the right.

The hike basically follows Tirbircio Creek up to its headwaters in the basin on the west side of the peak of Silver Mountain. However, the first half of the creek is in a sharp canyon most of the time. So from the Gold King Mill, hike north up an old road; it soon swings east and follows the creek (east southeast) but remains high above it. The road quits at an old mine after a mile and a quarter of steady climbing. Bushwhacking is required from this point, but it is not too difficult since you continue in the same basic direction. Silver Mountain is visible straight ahead most of the time. Before too long, you will emerge above timberline and have mostly talus the rest of the way.

As you work your way (in the same direction) up into the basin, turn left and climb 700 feet to a saddle between Silver Mountain and Baker Peak, which lies one mile northwest of Silver. It is lower at 11,949 feet. The climb up the saddle is steep and slow, but after that it is fairly easy to the top. Turn right at the saddle, and hike one-half mile southeast to the summit, which is another 750 feet higher.

From the top, you look (eastward) down into the headwaters of Lightner Creek, and much further beyond, Durango appears safely tucked into the Animas Valley. To the north and west are the many peaks of the La Plata Mountains. To the northeast on the distant skyline is Mountain View Crest and, just beyond, the Needles with three peaks above 14,000 feet. To the south is New Mexico. The top of Silver Mountain is a nice, smooth roll where you can be comfortable in taking leisurely views, if there is no wind.

The 5.3-mile round trip assumes return by the approach route, but there are two other alternatives.

One is Baker Peak. To do this, start back the way you came; at the saddle, continue northwest to the top of Baker in another quarter mile. There is an intermediate point of 150 feet to climb and descend before reaching Baker. From the top of Baker you get a fine view north to the next La Plata peak, Lewis Mountain. It is rocky and rough.

To descend from Baker, continue northwest along the ridge one-half mile to the beginning of timberline, then swing west down toward Tirbircio Creek. There is no trail in this area, but you should reach the old road that you ascended in about three quarters of a mile. From there on, it is simply a matter of following the road back to Gold King Mill.

The other alternate return from Silver is over Deadwood Mountain. It lies southwest of Silver via a connecting ridge just over one mile long. However, since the ridge is something of an S-curve, you start hiking off Silver northwest a quarter mile, then go southwest a half mile, and finally west another quarter mile to the top of Deadwood at 12,285 feet. To come off Deadwood, you can go straight north down a ridge or back east a couple of hundred yards to a little saddle and then north down a couloir into a small branch of Tirbircio Creek. Either route gives some steep territory near the top. In the couloir, a small branch of Tirbircio Creek starts; it will lead you back to the main creek in a mile. Those starting down the ridge can swing a little to the right after a half mile and join this branch or follow the ridge down about a mile and then swing to the right to Tirbircio itself. Most of this descent will be in the timber. Going all the way to the end of the ridge is apt to put you above some cliffs. Follow the creek down to the starting point.

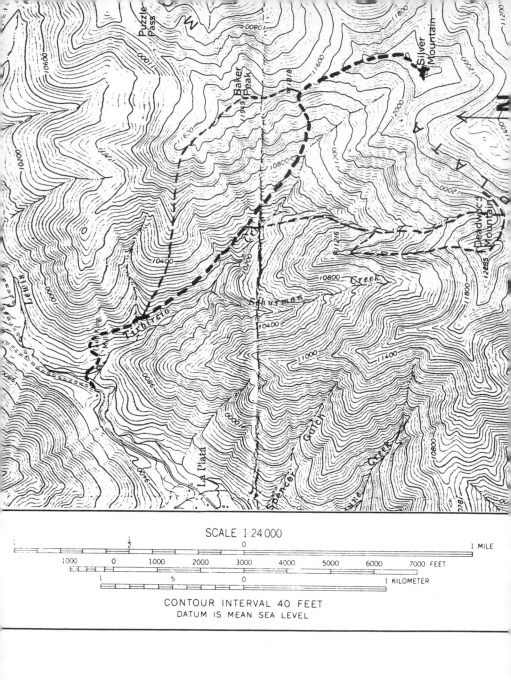

SCALE 1:24 000

CONTOUR INTERVAL 40 FEET
DATUM IS MEAN SEA LEVEL

70

Tomahawk Basin—Diorite Peak

Distance: 2 miles (round trip)
Starting Elevation: 10,900 feet
Elevation Gain: 1,861 feet
High Point: 12,761 feet
Rating: Moderate to hard
Time Allowed: 2½ to 3½ hours
Maps: 7½' La Plata
San Juan National Forest

This is another hike out of La Plata Canyon. It should not be attempted earlier than late July (except in years when the snowpack is below average) because of an avalanche path that usually fills La Plata Canyon Road not far above Lewis Creek. It takes a long time for the snow to melt and the forest service does not plow the road, but mining companies sometimes do.

To make this climb, take La Plata Canyon Road three miles north of Kroeger Campground, where there is a small parking area and a sign recommending only four-wheel drives beyond this point. The Gold King Mill is just across the river to the east. The road beyond this spot is rough, but two-wheel drives can usually make it one and three quarters miles up the road to the Tomahawk Basin turnoff.

The Tomahawk turnoff is sharply uphill to the left. The canyon road itself is narrow here. Two-wheel drives will need to park a little before or a little beyond the turnoff. Tomahawk Basin Road is very rough, steep, and narrow. Two-wheel drives should not attempt this road at all. Parking at the turnoff will add 1.6 miles (one way) and 1,000 feet of climb to the hike. Four-wheel drives can go up this 1.6 miles and park out of the way at the Tomahawk Mine.

The hike is without benefit of trail but is easy to follow because it quickly gets above timberline, where everything is visible. Above timberline, most of the hike is on loose talus rock.

Begin hiking north up the mountainside toward the low spot in the saddle. There will be a ridge running southeast on your right. A few hundred feet below the saddle is the site of an airplane crash from the early 1960s. This was a military flight in which two men were killed. The tragedy was all the more ironic since 300 feet more of altitude would have allowed them to clear the ridge. The crash and many snows have scattered the wreckage over a wide area. Most of it has been salvaged, but climbers will no doubt see some scraps of aluminum skin, wires, and other smaller parts as they climb through the area.

Once at the saddle, turn right, climb to the high point of the ridge, and follow it around northeast to Diorite. This is a half mile from the saddle.

The views from the top are breathtaking. Immediately below, steeply down on the west side, you look into Bear Creek Basin. This is wild country, not visited by many humans. On the far side of the basin are Mount Moss and Centennial Peak (formerly Banded Mountain). The connecting ridge between them is extremely rough and forbidding. Across this ridge and a little beyond is Hesperus Peak, at 13,232 feet, the highest point in the La Platas. North of Centennial, Sharkstooth rises steeply to a sharp point. To the north there is a complete panorama of peaks, including, from west to east, the San Miguels with their three fourteeners and the distinctive Lizard Head shaft, Grizzly Peak, Engineer Mountain, the Twilights, the Needles, and many more. To the east near at hand are La Plata Canyon and the east ridge of the La Plata Mountains.

Hikers should return by the same route that they ascended.

There is an alternate route you may want to consider which is easier and also offers the option of climbing Madden Peak and Parrott in the same trip. This route shows on the San Juan National Forest map but better on the topo maps; it lies principally on the 7½' Thompson Peak Quad topo. To take this route, drive to the top of Mancos Hill on Highway 160, just over halfway from Hesperus to the town of Mancos. At the top of the hill turn north on a gravel road into a fairly flat area; after a mile this road curves to the right and starts ascending. In another half mile the road splits; here take the left turn (the better road). The road goes on approximately another 3 miles, passing prominent radio towers a short distance to the left on a separate road. At this point the gravel stops at a cattle guard, but the road goes on. In wet weather two-wheel-drive vehicles may find it advisable to stop here. Others can go on most of another mile and park in a big meadow. Hiking should start by going on up this same road another half mile to another split in the road. Either branch of it can be taken from here. The left fork takes you to the top of a ridge where you should turn right off the road and follow the ridge directly to the summit of Madden Peak (11,972 ft.), in about a mile. There is a trail along much of this ridge; it is an easy climb. To do Parrott from there go down a ridge to the right (about ninety degrees from the ascent ridge). This is a little east of straight south. Here you drop down to a saddle at 11,560 ft. before ascending another 300 ft. to the top of Parrott. If you choose the right fork of the road at the split you will stay in a basin below the Madden ridge and head straight for the saddle; this is mostly east with a little bias to the north. It is basically easy going. At the saddle you have a choice as to which peak to do first. Madden is to the left, Parrot to the right. You can easily do either one or both.

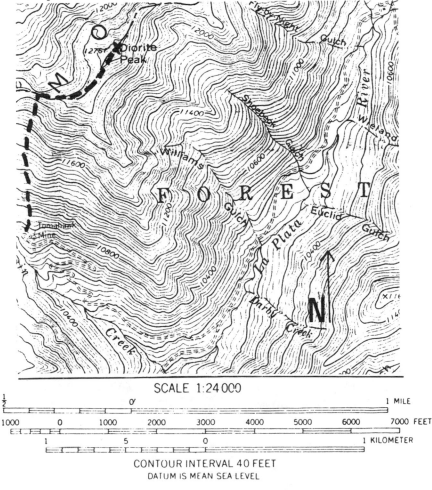

SCALE 1:24 000

CONTOUR INTERVAL 40 FEET
DATUM IS MEAN SEA LEVEL

Centennial Peak and Sharkstooth

Distance: 4.4 miles (add .5 miles for Sharkstooth)
round trip
Starting Elevation: 10,900 feet
Elevation Gain: 2,162 feet (plus 526 feet for
Sharkstooth)
High Point: 13,062 feet
Rating: Centennial — moderate; Sharkstooth — hard
Time Allowed: 3 hours to Centennial and back.
(From Durango this is an all-day trip because of
the long drive.)
Maps: 7½ ' La Plata
San Juan National Forest

This hike is described as a climb to the top of Centennial Peak with an optional side trip to the top of Sharkstooth.

A fairly long drive is involved; the last eight miles of it are through tall aspen forest with occasional breaks in the trees to reveal the western profile of the La Platas. These are the highest peaks in the range but are not often seen because lower peaks block the view from all directions except west. This territory is unpopulated for a number of miles. As you approach from the west, the glimpses that you get are of Hesperus (at 13,232 feet, the highest peak in the La Platas), Moss, Spiller, Centennial, and Sharkstooth; all except Sharkstooth are over 13,000 feet. While it is a bit shorter, it captures your attention because of its sharp triangular shape thrusting abruptly into the sky above the pass. From this angle it definitely looks like a shark's tooth.

To take this hike, go north out of Mancos on the Dolores road, State Highway 184. Just a quarter mile north of Mancos, turn right uphill on the road marked for Jackson Reservoir and Transfer Campground. At eleven miles from Mancos, turn right on the Transfer Campground and Windy Gap road. At about seven and one-half miles down this road, you should find a little side road angling off to the right; there is a sign on it with an arrow pointing to "Sharkstooth Trail." This road takes you one and one-half miles, past Twin Lakes, to the trailhead. This road is rough and, in places, rocky. It is best made in a four-wheel-drive vehicle, but other cars can make it when the road is dry if the driver pays attention to clearance over rocks.

At the trailhead, the road turns sharply right, and there is room here to park several cars.

The trail begins in big spruce and fir and moves steadily uphill to the saddle between Sharkstooth and Centennial. This is an easy and well-defined trail. Part way up is an old mine on the left. Near this same area, at the south end of a switchback, is a breathtaking view of Hesperus Peak on the right and Centennial on the left. A very jagged ridge and an unnamed peak are in between.

Centennial is a bit shorter than Hesperus and is distinguished from the sharper peaks by a roll top. Both Centennial and Hesperus are characterized by bands of different-colored sedimentary rocks. In fact, Centennial was called Banded Mountain until its name was officially changed July 30, 1976, in celebration of the Colorado state centennial. This was, of course, the same month in which the United States was celebrating its bicentennial. This mountain is listed on the La Plata quad map as Banded Mountain. Unfortunately, the national forest map does not show it at all; however, it does show Sharkstooth, which is lower. Therefore, you can find the location on the forest map about one mile south of Sharkstooth.

Now back to the route description. At the saddle, turn south (right) off the trail, which at that point goes east and drops deeply down into Bear Creek Canyon. When you turn right, there is no more trail to follow, but you cannot get lost—just climb upward seven-tenths mile to the summit. You start up steeply over talus; after 150 yards you come to a much more gradual slope over tundra. Stay near the high point of the ridge. As you get near the top, it will be rocky again. There are some paths showing in this area.

Each time I have climbed this mountain there has been a strong, cold west wind; it seems to be a regular pattern for the area. Be sure to have warm clothes along, including gloves, even in the summer. My first climb of Centennial was during the last week of December. There was not much snow that year, only four to six inches on the exposed parts of the mountain and less below. But in spite of the fact that it was a beautiful sunny day, the members of our group nearly froze because of the bitterly cold wind. Fortunately, at the top we only had to take a few steps down to a ledge on the east side to complete shelter from the

Climbing Centennial from the saddle on the trail with Sharkstooth in the background.

wind. Here we ate lunch and viewed the scenery in comfort. One of the first men to the top had thoughtfully brought along his little propane pack stove and had hot bouillon ready to serve the freezing later arrivals—just the right thing at the right time and place.

The views from the top are excellent in all directions except south, where the neighboring peaks are the whole view. To the southeast toward Durango you cannot quite see the city, but you can see Fort Lewis College, which is located on a mesa 300 feet above Durango on its east side. To the north you can see the full sweep of the San Juans, from the Needles northeast to the San Miguels northwest. Even further west are the Blues in Utah, and to the southwest the Sleeping Ute.

The return trip should be made to the saddle and back down the trail that you ascended.

The climb up Centennial Peak is not really difficult, but talus and the altitude make it deserve a moderate rating.

If you wish to climb Sharkstooth on this same excursion, simply attack its south side from the saddle. It is only 526 feet above the saddle, but it is much more difficult than Centennial. It starts over ordinary talus but gets steeper and steeper as you rise. There are plenty of rocks to grab, but the trouble is that most of them are loose, and it is very easy to start a rock slide. No member of a climbing party should be immediately below another. Near the top, every handhold and foothold must be tested for solidity before trusting your weight to it.

The top is very small, and the north face drops even more precipitously than the south face. The views are much the same as from Centennial. The descent must be done with even more care than the ascent because of the longer reach of the legs and the loose rocks.

This climb is short and quick. (I made it to the top in twenty minutes from the saddle.) But it must be rated hard because of the loose rock hazard.

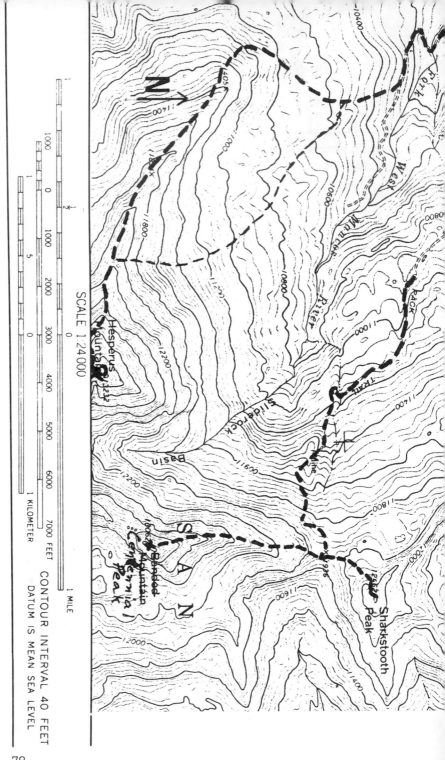

SCALE 1:24 000

1000   0   1000   2000   3000   4000   5000   6000   7000 FEET

1   0   1   5   1 KILOMETER

1   0   1 MILE

CONTOUR INTERVAL 40 FEET
DATUM IS MEAN SEA LEVEL

78

Hesperus Mountain

Distance: 5 miles (round trip)
Starting Elevation: 10,080 feet
Elevation Gain: 3,152 feet
High Point: 13,232 feet
Rating: Difficult
Time Allowed: 4 to 6 hours

Maps: 7½ ' La Plata
    San Juan National Forest

Hesperus Peak is the highest point in the La Plata Mountains. It makes a good one-day hike and climb; its summit gives almost a complete 360-degree view. To the south and southeast, nearby peaks cut off some valley views. Hesperus is a handsome mountain and well worth the climb. It is not seen very often except at considerable distance, and this is mainly from the west. The eastern and southern parts of the La Platas and other San Juan peaks cut off views of it from the populated areas and highways.

The peak is to be climbed from the west ridge. This can be done from the north or the south side of the ridge. The south side is approached via the Echo Basin road two miles east of Mancos. The more usual route is by the north side of the ridge; this route is described here.

Take Colorado State Highway 184 (the Dolores road) north out of Mancos one quarter mile; then turn east (right) uphill on the road marked for Jackson Lake and Transfer Campground. At eleven miles north of Mancos, turn east (right) on the road marked for Transfer Park and Windy Gap. About five miles farther, turn right on a little road leading to the North Fork of the West Mancos River. Drive about one and one-half miles to where a bridge is out, and park there. This last road is very rough. Those with two-wheel-drive vehicles may have to park before the end of the road and hike the rest of it.

There are usually some logs or beams across the stream where the bridge was. Cross here, and start the ascent south. There is no trail, but some old logging roads are useful for a little way. Above these, move south up the hillside through a band of

Hesperus Mountain from the western approach road. Centennial Peak is off its left shoulder and Sharkstooth at the far left.

big timber that is less than a quarter mile wide. From here, you will emerge into open talus at the west end of the west ridge of the mountain. Some of this is quite steep and tends to move under footsteps. The nearer the west end of the ridge you are, the easier it will be, but you cannot avoid all of the steepness. Once on top of this ridge, you will find it much easier going for some distance as you turn east and follow the ridge toward the peak. Most of this area is tundra with a few short, bushy conifers. After crossing this area, you come to what has appeared at a distance to be a big red shoulder, but the left side of this offers a steep, though quite usable route. Beyond this stay to the right of the ridge, and move on up to the summit. Part of the time you will be on loose rock, part of the time on a ledge. The top is not large but is enough of a roll to support several people comfortably as they eat their well-earned sandwiches and absorb the great panorama. There are connecting ridges to Mount Moss southeast and to Centennial northeast. The one to Centennial looks essentially impossible to cross; the other one may be negotiable, though I have not tried it.

The return route is the same as the approach for this hike. However, a little way to the west of the red ledge there is, in the early summer, a snowy chute that can provide a good glissade for those equipped with ice axes and proper experience. The top of this is quite steep and can be hazardous for the novice. It does offer a quick and exciting way down the steep part of the ridge.

Because of the talus, the steepness, and the total altitude gain, this hike is rated difficult. However, most anyone in good health and with patience and some carefulness should be able to make it and enjoy it.

Glissading off Hesperus.

Parrott Peak

Distance: 6 miles (round trip)
Starting Elevation: 8,600 feet
Elevation Gain: 3,257 feet
High Point: 11,857 feet
Rating: Moderate
Time Allowed: 5 hours
Maps: 7½' Hesperus
        7½' La Plata
        San Juan National Forest

This is an interesting climb in the fall, when higher areas are snowed in. It has the advantage of a southern exposure, which keeps the snow off later in the fall and takes it off earlier in the spring. It is also quickly accessible from Durango. The described route requires a four-wheel-drive to get to the starting point, but this only involves an extra two miles (each way) for those with two-wheel-drive transportation. This would also add an extra 440 feet of altitude gain.

To reach this area, drive west of Durango on Highway 160, 5.6 miles west of Hesperus to the Cherry Creek National Forest Campground. Just beyond the campground, a little four-wheel-drive road turns north uphill through a gate (which is normally either open or not locked). Two-wheel-drive vehicles can make it part way up this road when it is dry, but it climbs steeply in places and has a couple of very rough spots. At one mile, this road reaches an old railroad right-of-way. Turn right and follow this east one and one-half miles. There is a side route here that will allow you to drive a short distance uphill, where you can park in a clearing near the timber.

The hike is basically bushwhacking, although there are some trails from time to time that can be followed profitably. They are not official national forest trails and are not maintained. They are just paths maintained by traffic, both bovine and human.

An interesting feature that you may want to hike around lies just east along the railroad right-of-way. It is a large landslide area involving many acres. It is not in the steep area but the flatter level below the steep part. It is a very chewed-up piece of land with lots of cracks and ups and downs. The right-of-way is dislocated so that you cannot drive on it any farther.

For the climb, head north through the timber. After a mile and a quarter, the going gets quite steep. This lasts a little over one-half mile and brings you to the top of a partially cleared ridge. The actual top is another mile northwest along this ridge, most of it easy hiking. The top is above timberline and affords fine views down into La Plata Canyon and across the canyon to the eastern range of the La Plata peaks. There are also good views south to the mesa country and on into New Mexico.

The return trip should follow the same general route as the approach. There is nothing really difficult on this trip, but the total altitude gain is substantial; therefore, the trip is rated moderate.

The route can be made a little easier but slightly longer by driving another quarter mile beyond the Tomahawk Mine to the Little Kate Mine, where there is generous parking space. At this point begin hiking up and right on what appears at first to be a drivable road, but it soon ceases to be so. This route zigzags upward a half mile and stops at an upper mine. From here a trail goes on up toward the saddle on the ridge, zigzagging on the way. The trail stops below the ridge, but a short scramble completes that part. Once on the ridge turn right and follow on up to the false summit and beyond a short distance to the top of Diorite. This route reduces the altitude to be gained through hiking by 200 feet.

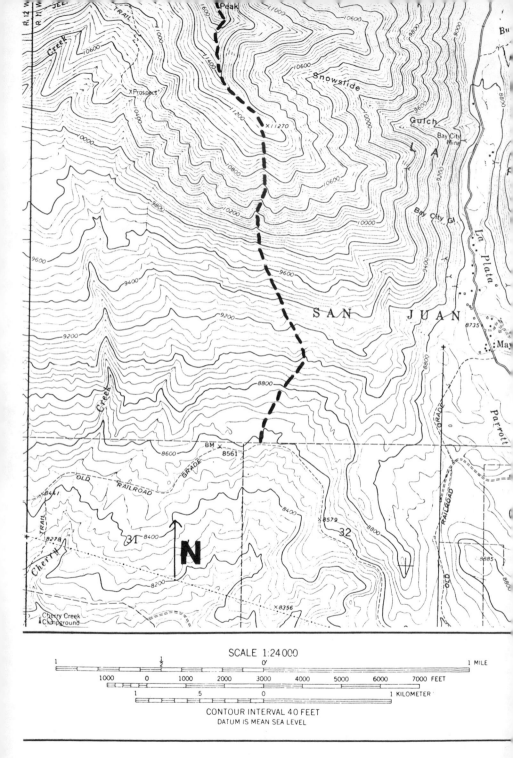

SCALE 1:24 000

CONTOUR INTERVAL 40 FEET
DATUM IS MEAN SEA LEVEL

Gibbs Peak

Distance: 2 miles (round trip)
Starting Elevation: 10,850 feet
Elevation Gain: 1,436 feet
High Point: 12,286 feet
Rating: Moderate
Time Allowed: 1 ½ to 2 hours
Maps: 7½ ' La Plata
San Juan National Forest

Gibbs Peak is in the La Plata Mountains northwest of Durango. From the top of the four-wheel-drive road to the summit involves only about one mile of climbing. As high peaks go, it is fairly easy, but it is rated moderate because much of the hike requires steep walking.

The approach is made via La Plata Canyon, a beautiful drive in itself. To get there, take U.S. Highway 160 west out of Durango eleven miles. One-quarter mile beyond the Hesperus turnoff, take a right turn (north). This road starts off as blacktop; in four miles, just beyond the mining town of Mayday, it becomes gravel and enters La Plata Canyon, following along the west side of the La Plata River. Two miles further is Kroeger Campground. This is a lovely place to camp if you are so minded. It is set in the flat among big trees with easy access to the river; it is a good launching place for hiking, jeeping, fishing, and picnicking. Kroeger is a Forest Service campground. The whole canyon is a popular place in the summer, with rugged high peaks on each side, lingering snow until July, many high waterfalls, big spruce, fir and aspen trees, and some of the most prolific wild flowers to be found anywhere.

For the Gibbs Peak climb, go another mile and a half beyond Kroeger Campground, and turn left uphill on a little side road just before crossing Bedrock Creek. Two-wheel-drive cars should park one and one-half miles up this road where the road goes straight on to the Allard Mine. At this point, four-wheel drives should make a sharp left turn and go on up the hill. (Those who must start hiking here should follow the same road. It adds 1.4 miles and 750 feet of altitude.) The parking place for four-wheel drives is at the end of a half-mile straight stretch in the road, just below the top of a ridge. The road switches back left at this point, but vehicles cannot go much farther. Parking gets difficult above this point.

Begin hiking on up the road. It makes a couple of switchbacks and soon runs into trees down across the road. It is possible to follow the road further around and up the hillside, but it is shorter just to start climbing west up the mountainside toward the top. There is no trail, but you should not get lost as long as you are going up. The forest here is not very cluttered with brush and downed timber. In a few hundred yards, you emerge above timberline and climb on loose rocks most of the rest of the way. Just before the top, there is a short distance of scrambling over firm rocky ledges. Once over this, you just follow the roll top southwest to the highest point.

The west ridge of the La Platas is a bit higher than the east ridge. Gibbs Peak is about 1,000 feet lower than the highest of the west ridge peaks, but it affords fine views to the south, where nothing is higher. In this direction, you can see all the way into New Mexico and Arizona. Seventy-five miles south and a little west is Shiprock, a distinctive stone shaft pointing skyward. It is an ancient volcanic plug that thrusts 1,800 feet above its surrounding terrain. It is a very sacred place to the Navajos. This should be quite visible from Gibbs except on very hazy or cloudy days.

Eastward from Gibbs, you get a complete survey of La Plata Canyon and the east range of the La Plata Mountains; it is rugged and beautiful country. Westward is the East Mancos River valley, and beyond lie the towns of Mancos and Cortez. In the distance and a bit north are the Blue and La Sal mountains near Monticello and Moab, Utah. To the north, and near at hand, are the highest peaks of the La Platas.

The hike planned here returns by the approach route. However, ambitious hikers with plenty of time may want to add the challenge of Burwell Peak. At 12,664 feet it is 378 feet higher than Gibbs. Those who try this should exercise due care, for there are some rough spots in the mile of ridge that leads northeast from Gibbs to Burwell, including some precipitous drops off the east side. Another half mile beyond Burwell lies Spiller Peak at 13,123 feet, one of five La Plata peaks that rise above 13,000 feet. Babcock, another thirteener, is next in line, but it should not be approached from this side.

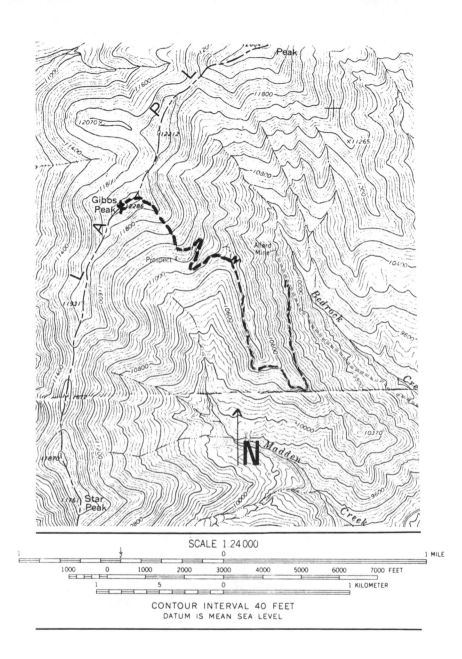

SCALE 1:24000

CONTOUR INTERVAL 40 FEET
DATUM IS MEAN SEA LEVEL

Hiking on Hermosa Trail.

CHAPTER 5

Hikes Between
Durango and Silverton

Hermosa Trail

Distance: 8 miles (round trip), with additional options.
Starting Elevation: 7,800 feet
Elevation Gain: 200 feet
High Point: 8,000 feet
Rating: Easy
Time Allowed: 3½ to 4½ hours
Maps: 7½' Hermosa
   7½' Monument Hill
   7½' Elk Creek
   San Juan National Forest

Hermosa Trail is in the heart of a very large roadless area. There are high ridges and many canyons. The whole area contains many thousands of acres. The main trail is twenty miles long, and there are many side trails. To explore this area with any degree of thoroughness would take weeks of backpacking, so most of this region lies beyond the scope of this book. However, good day and half-day hikes can be done from the south end quite easily.

This is excellent elk-hunting territory and has good trout streams as well. There are also many deer.

The trail at first follows the contour of Hermosa Creek but is several hundred feet above it so that you look down into the canyon below and up at the heavily wooded mountains. Across the canyon, the hills rise up above timberline to the thirteen-thousand-foot peaks of the La Platas.

The trail is one of the widest, best maintained, and most heavily used in southwestern Colorado. It is also one of the easiest to hike, for there is no major altitude change. Along the trail are big trees, open vistas, and wild flowers.

To get to the trail, take U.S. Highway 550 ten miles north of Durango to Hermosa Village. Just north of the bridge over Hermosa Creek, and before the railroad crossing, turn left on a little side road. In a distance of just several yards, this road meets a north-south road that parallels the highway. Turn right (north) here, and follow this road uphill to its end in four miles. The first half or more of it is blacktop and the rest gravel. At the dead end, park off to the side and begin the hike just off the end of the road. The trail goes sharply down for about twenty yards, then meets the main trail, which you should take to the right. This point should be carefully studied and remembered for the sake of the return trip, because it is easy to miss this "exit ramp." A miss takes you not only past your car, but quickly onto private property.

The main trail crosses several side streams that may be fairly well dried up, or they may be flowing and muddy, making hiking boots useful, though not needed on other parts of the trail.

At four miles, the trail divides. This is where the options begin. The left branch descends 500 feet in the next mile to a good footbridge across Dutch Creek. Just beyond here, you can step off to the left to Hermosa Creek itself. Both of these are good fishing streams. Hiking beyond this brings you back up to the previous level. You can continue on as far as interest and time permit.

If you take the right branch at the trail split, you are on the Dutch Creek Trail, though you do not see the creek itself until you go up the trail a mile. There is one fairly steep hill of about 250 feet that you go down before reaching the creek. Again, you can hike on this trail as far as time and interest permit. There is a

90

small open grassy meadow where you first come to the stream.

Whichever trail you take, return by the same route to the road and your parking place.

All of this area is excellent for elk. An especially good place to look for them is in the aspen trees at the beginning of Dutch Creek Trail.

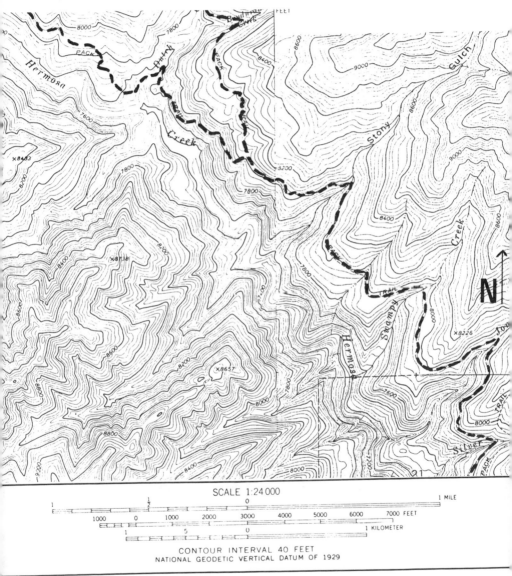

SCALE 1:24 000

CONTOUR INTERVAL 40 FEET
NATIONAL GEODETIC VERTICAL DATUM OF 1929

Mitchell Lakes

*Distance: 8 miles (round trip) to top of
the ridge above the lakes*
Starting Elevation: 6,800 feet
Elevation Gain: 2,600 feet
High Point: 9,400 feet
Rating: Moderate
Time Allowed: 4½ to 5½ hours
Maps: 7½' Hermosa
      San Juan National Forest

Mitchell Lakes as such are not much to brag about. There
are four little lakes in the group. They are shallow and filled with
marsh grass, but they occupy a secluded shelf surrounded by
meadow, which, in turn, is surrounded by Ponderosa pine and
some aspen. There are perhaps one hundred acres of open
space; here you can get a feeling of both spaciousness and in-
sulation from the rest of the world. The hike itself yields rewarding views of the Animas Valley and Missionary Ridge beyond.

To take this hike, follow U.S. Highway 550 thirteen miles
north of Durango, to a right turn downhill toward Baker's Bridge.
You soon come to the old highway. Turn left on it (north) a little
way to the first left turn. This is a dirt road and leads back west
under the new highway through a large steel tube. This soon
becomes a very rough four-wheel-drive road. In fact, a four-
wheel-drive vehicle could go all the way to the lakes, but it is not
recommended since the road is very rough and, in places, very
steep. It is preferable to park back on the old highway or just off
it before going under the new highway.

Begin hiking at this point. You soon cross the narrow gauge
Durango-to-Silverton railroad track. Follow the road all the way
to the lakes area, which is three miles.

The distance and elevation gain given in the heading for this
hike take you a mile beyond the lakes to the top of the ridge. To
go on from the lakes, hike north between the two most northerly
lakes a little ways up the hillside, where you will strike an abandoned jeep trail. Take it left up to the ridge top.

From here, you can see eastward down into the valley to

Shalona and Stratton lakes and west down into Hermosa Creek valley and up to the La Platas. This is a great forested, roadless area. If you desire, you can hike northwest along the ridge top for several miles. There is a good trail. In two and one-half miles, you will strike Jones Creek Trail. If you take it left downhill, you will strike Hermosa Road in three and a quarter miles at Big Spring Creek. This point is four miles above the Hermosa settlement and U.S. Highway 550.

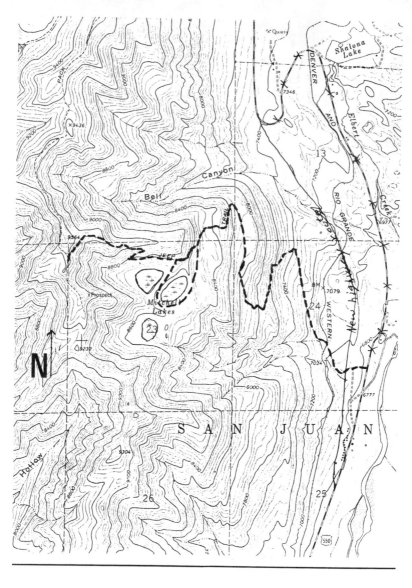

SCALE 1:24 000

1   1/2   0'   1 MILE

1000   0   1000   2000   3000   4000   5000   6000   7000 FEET

1   5   0   1 KILOMETER

CONTOUR INTERVAL 40 FEET
DATUM IS MEAN SEA LEVEL

Goulding Creek

Distance: 6 miles (round trip)
Starting Elevation: 7,880 feet
Elevation Gain: 2,190 feet
High Point: 10,070 feet
Rating: Moderate
Time Allowed: 3½ to 4½ hours
Maps: 7½' Electra Lake
San Juan National Forest

Ten miles north of Durango a series of high bluffs begins on the west side of U.S. Highway 550. These bluffs, known as Hermosa Cliffs, continue on north for sixteen miles. In places they are precipitous and look invulnerable. But they can be breached via three good trails. Near the south end, ahead of the genuine cliffs, is the Mitchell Lakes Trail; near the middle is Goulding Creek; and near the north end is Elbert Creek.

Goulding approaches from an area that looks nearly impossible from below, but it turns out to be a very good trail and not terribly steep, thanks to many switchbacks. It is a trail satisfactory for horses. Horse-riding hunters use it in the fall and cattlemen through the summer.

The trail is located seventeen miles north of Durango and leads off U.S. Highway 550. The trail is about one mile north of the main gate of the Tamarron resort on the opposite (west) side of the road. You take a turnoff here where you can drive in a quarter mile to grassy parking. The trail starts west looking like a four-wheel-drive road, but it quickly narrows to a trail and swings south above Tamarron's water supply tank. It soon moves westward again and mounts rapidly through a series of switchbacks up through a beautiful aspen grove. At some points, there are open spots in the trees that provide good views of the valley below and Missionary Ridge beyond. This is a beautiful hike at any time, but it is especially lovely during late September and early October, when the aspen leaves are at their golden best.

This trail is always slightly above Goulding Creek until you break through the Hermosa Cliffs at about one mile up the trail and a thousand feet of altitude gain.

When you get through the cliffs, you are ushered into a peaceful green valley surrounded by tall timber on the hillsides. This is only a mile from the highway (less in a straight line), but it is a different world, one inhabited by curious herefords and freedom-loving elk and deer. A couple of old log cabins are located in the valley. One seems to be basically a hunter's camp and the other a shelter sometimes used by cattle.

You soon come close to the stream after arriving in the valley, but the water is not recommended for drinking without purification, unless you are early enough in the summer to be ahead of the cows. Goulding Creek during much of the summer is just a trickling stream; it sometimes ceases to flow altogether.

For a short hike, you could terminate here, but it is worth going on. The trail beyond is a little harder to follow because of the many cow paths, but with a bit of care, you should not have much trouble. The main trail stays fairly close to the stream most of the time, moving northwest to the top of the ridge, where it ends by joining the Jones Creek Trail, a north-south trail at the crest of the ridge.

The last quarter mile to the top is surrounded by acres and acres of lupine. During much of the summer, beginning quite early, this is a sea of blue floral display, well worth the hike by itself.

At the top, you look westward down into the Dutch Creek drainage and on across the vast Hermosa Creek roadless area. This is one of the best elk summering grounds in southwest Colorado.

The three miles given in the heading presuppose a return back down the same trail. But those who want a long hike have a couple of other options. Either of these would mean coming out at or near the end of the Hermosa Road, where you would need another car or someone to pick you up, for you would be nearly fifteen miles by road from the original parking place.

The first and shortest optional return is to go left down Jones Creek Trail. It follows the ridge about three miles before descending along Jones Creek for another three miles to the Hermosa Road.

The second option is via the Dutch Creek Trail. The easy but long way to join this trail is to go right (north) up the Jones Creek Trail two miles to where the Dutch Creek Trail joins it from the west. It is about six and one-half miles down this trail to the Hermosa Trail and another five miles down (left, or southeast) that trail to the Hermosa Road.

Another option, saving three miles, is to go west downhill where Goulding joins Jones Creek. This requires bushwhacking, but it is only a mile between the two trails this way, and you join Dutch Creek two miles lower down than by hiking north to the trail intersection.

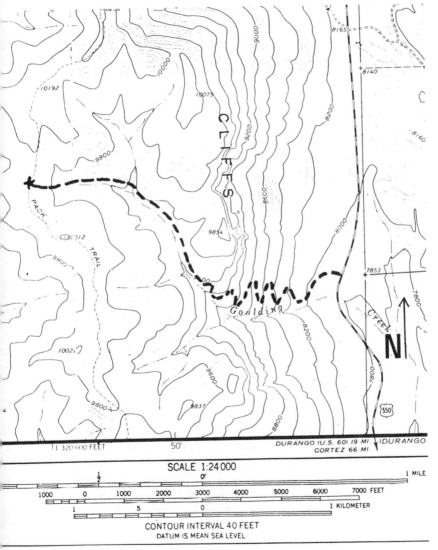

SCALE 1:24 000

CONTOUR INTERVAL 40 FEET
DATUM IS MEAN SEA LEVEL

Elbert Creek

Distance: 9 miles (round trip)
Starting Elevation: 8,800 feet
Elevation Gain: 1,650 feet
High Point: 10,450 feet
Rating: Easy, but long
Time Allowed: 4 to 6 hours
Maps: 7½ ' Electra Lake
7½ ' Elk Creek
San Juan National Forest

The Elbert Creek Trail breaks through the Hermosa Cliffs four miles south of Purgatory Ski Area, or twenty-three miles north of Durango on U.S. Highway 550. The trailhead is a little difficult to locate, but the trail soon becomes well defined beyond its beginning. It starts just south of the boundary of Needles Country Store and goes west along the south side of a fence. In a quarter mile you come to Elbert Creek. It is a good-sized stream and can be a problem for crossing, especially in late spring when the snowmelt is still coming down. It has to be crossed higher up also, but the first crossing is the only difficult one. You may elect just to wade it.

The hike itself is not difficult. The trail soon enters a deep canyon that makes its way through the Hermosa Cliffs and rises quite gradually through big timber in four and one-half miles to the top of the ridge that separates this drainage from the Hermosa drainage. It is a good trail most of the way. At one point, it joins and follows a road for a few hundred yards. It follows along the south side of the creek at this point. You should be able to pick it up again where the road turns north to cross the creek. It is another one and one-half miles to the top of the ridge.

This hike description only takes you to the top of this ridge; the return is by the same route. The trail, however, goes on down the other side and joins the Hermosa Trail in another six and one-half miles. This route is not recommended unless you are prepared to stay overnight, but it is another five miles north to the closest road, the Hermosa Park Road.

The road that you cross before reaching the top of the ridge is a good dirt road. It is possible to terminate the hike there, only three miles from its beginning. This road is reached from the Purgatory Ski Area. To get to it, turn off U.S. Highway 550 at the ski area turnoff. Just as you arrive at the east end of the Purgatory parking area, turn right; this road goes above Purgatory in a series of switchbacks to the top of the ridge. Where this road turns right in a flat spot, take a left turn instead. In about five miles of twisting road, you come to the spot where the Elbert Creek Trail joins it. This road is on the whole pretty good, and two-wheel-drive vehicles can use it when it is dry, though there are a few rough spots. Those who want an easy hike could drive to this point and hike down.

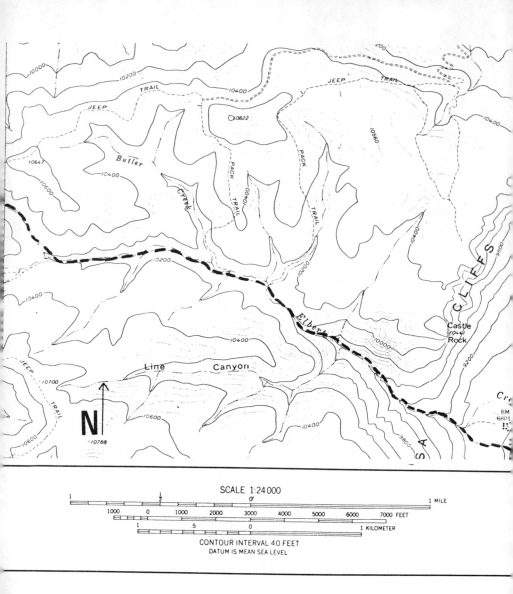

SCALE 1:24 000

CONTOUR INTERVAL 40 FEET
DATUM IS MEAN SEA LEVEL

Four Base Lake

Distance: *3 miles (round trip)*
Starting Elevation: *8,120 feet*
Elevation Gain: *160 feet*
High Point: *8,280 feet*
Rating: *Easy*
Time Allowed: *1 ½ hours*
Maps: *7½ ' Electra Lake*

This is a very easy hike with little elevation change along a four-wheel-drive road. It passes through rather dense vegetation, which makes it a bit unique in this part of the state. Four Base Lake is a good fishing place. It has been a supply lake for Tacoma power plant but is currently being bypassed for that purpose.

To get to the starting point for this hike, take U.S. Highway 550 eighteen miles north of Durango to a right turn (east) on the Haviland Lake Road. Haviland Lake is a lovely larger lake with a nice forest service campground and good fishing. Drive in from the highway about a mile; shortly after crossing the bridge at the southeast corner of Haviland, you should be able to find parking room. Four-wheel-drive vehicles could drive all the way to Four Base Lake, but the road is too rough for other vehicles. Anyway, it is a lovely hike.

After parking, continue hiking east from Haviland. A road goes north here, but that leads up into the camping area. Along much of the hike you will be following a big pipe that carries the water supply for Tacoma from Electra Lake a mile further north. (Electra Lake is a large and attractive place but is not open to the public.)

Just southeast of Four Base, you can stand at the top of the bluff overlooking the Animas River and the power plant a thousand feet below. At the right time of day in the summer, you might even see the little narrow gauge train at the bottom of the canyon carrying sightseers between Durango and Silverton.

Across the Animas Valley, the view is up the steep, high western side of Missionary Ridge.

101

The road stops at Four Base, so the return will need to be made back up the way you came.

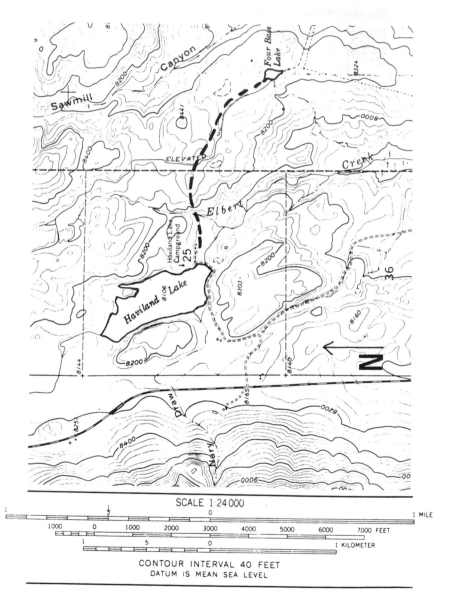

SCALE 1:24000

CONTOUR INTERVAL 40 FEET
DATUM IS MEAN SEA LEVEL

Molas Trail

Distance: 8 miles (round trip)
Starting Elevation: 10,604 feet
Elevation Gain: 1,674 feet
High Point: 10,604 feet
Rating: Easy to Moderate
Time Allowed: 3 ½ to 4 ½ hours
Maps: 7 ½ ' Snowden Peak
San Juan National Forest

This is a good trail and offers a very fine half-day hike with excellent views of the Animas Canyon. Most hikes in this guide start at the low point and climb to a high point. This hike is the opposite; it starts at the high point and goes down to the low point at the river, which is at 8,930 feet. The elevation gain is on the return trip.

This trail starts off the east side of U.S. Highway 550 about six miles south of Silverton, one and one-half miles north of Molas Pass. There is a good turnout with a parking area south of Molas Lake (not to be confused with Little Molas Lake, one-half mile further south and on the west side of the road). Do not stop at Molas Lake itself—it is a small, commercialized piece of private property.

The trail begins across the road from the parking area and moves south, curving eastward in a quarter mile past a sheep camp and down a hill. As soon as you cross the low point, usually a dry stream, there is some difficulty following the trail. If you continue east with some bias to the south, you should pick it up again moving over a little rise. Molas Creek should be several hundred yards to the right (as you face east). The trail is distinct down through the rocky east side of this rise. It leads down and eastward across an open meadow with an aspen grove on the left. If you are in the aspens, you will need to move south down a steep slope covered with aspen. At the bottom, the trail is quite distinct and is excellent the rest of the way to the river.

After crossing the flat meadow, you plunge into big spruce-fir timber. Shortly, the trail begins a series of switchbacks leading down to the river one thousand feet below. Here and there, a break in the trees affords a dramatic view of the canyon below. The river winds its way through the bottom, with the railroad track paralleling it on the east side.

Mount Garfield stands stalwart guard above the east side of the valley, while further south, the peak Fourteen massif seems to block off the whole canyon and reach all the way to the sky. In mid-afternoon you have a good chance of seeing one of the two tourist trains seeking its way south toward Durango. At the south end of the visible part of the valley, the train often stops to take on backpackers from Elk Creek.

There are several gorgeous views of the valley from different levels as you swing back and forth in your descent. At the bottom, you cross Molas Creek and soon emerge from the high vegetation to find a fine bridge across the Animas River for hikers and horses.

This is the destination point for the hike described here, since this guide does not cover the Weminuche Wilderness. But if you are backpacking, you can cross the railroad track and go down a little to find the Elk Creek Trail up the east side of the canyon and to the top of the continental divide in another 8.2 miles.

For this hike, it is a matter of turning around and going back the way you came, and, of course, this is where the work begins as you ascend what you came down so easily. However, the climb out of the canyon can be rated easy to moderate, since none of the many switchbacks are steep.

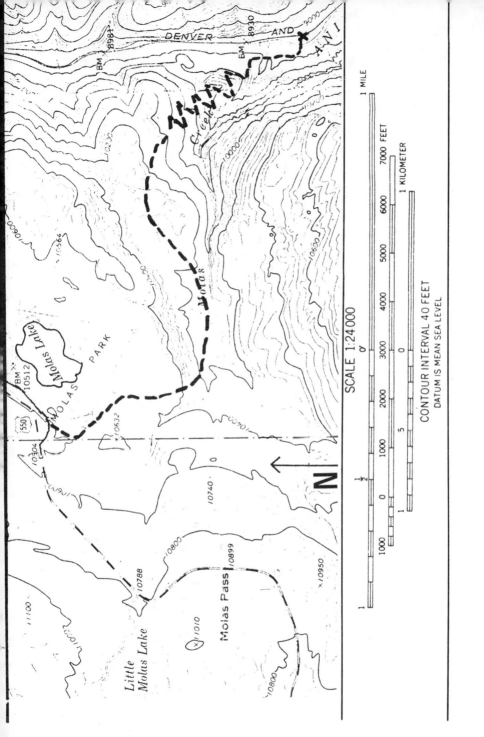

SCALE 1:24 000

CONTOUR INTERVAL 40 FEET
DATUM IS MEAN SEA LEVEL

105

Purgatory Trail

Distance: 8 miles (round trip)
Starting Elevation: 8,800 feet
Elevation Gain: 1,100 feet
Rating: Easy to moderate
Time Allowed: 3½ to 4½ hours
Maps: 7½' Engineer Mountain
7½' Electra Lake
San Juan National Forest

This hike is another reverse climb, where you begin at the top, hike down to the river below (at 7,700 feet), then climb back out of the canyon. This is a good half-day hike, but the views, which are great by many standards, are not quite so dramatic as those afforded by the Molas Trail into the same canyon several miles upstream. Cascade Canyon is deep and narrow with a rugged beauty all its own.

This trail starts out of the northeast side of the Purgatory Campground. Parking is available west across the highway. The campground is located twenty-eight miles north of Durango just south of the Purgatory Ski Area turnoff.

The trail moves eastward from the campground and soon begins to descend rapidly. In one mile, it turns south and moves along Purgatory Flats for about three-fourths mile, where it comes right along Cascade Creek just as the creek is about to enter its narrow canyon in its final plunge to the river. Most of the hike is close to the west side of Cascade, but it sometimes moves up to 250 feet above the stream in search of an adequate bench. At the end, the trail zigzags back and forth down to the river just below the mouth of Cascade Creek. Here is a nice flat area on both sides of the river for resting and picnicking. The east side is larger than the west and has some good tree coverage. There is a good bridge for hikers and horses.

At this point, the planned half-day hike returns back up the same trail. The trail itself, for backpackers, continues north along the east side of the river, always near to it, for another five and one-half miles, where it joins the Columbine Pass Trail, which, in turn, takes you on up to Chicago Basin and Columbine Pass.

This is an easy to moderate hike but does have over one thousand feet of altitude gain on the return.

Looking out of Cascade Canyon along Purgatory Trail with Engineer Mountain in the distance.

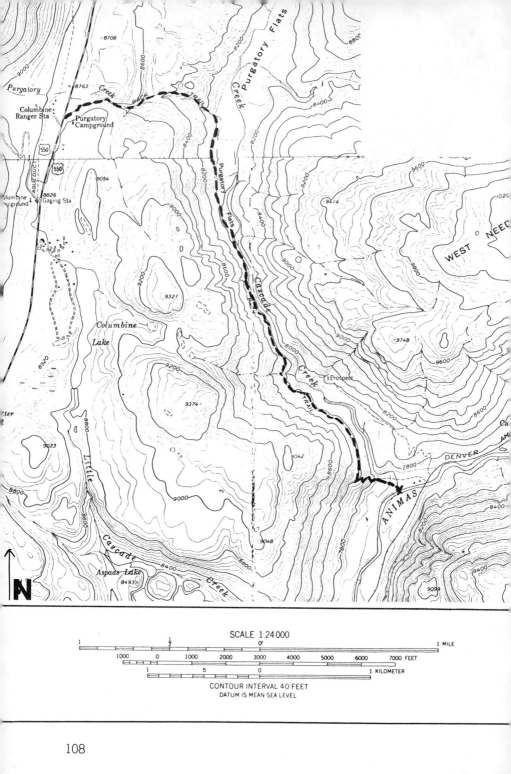

Potato (Spud) Lake

Distance: 2 miles (round trip)
Starting Elevation: 9,360 feet
Elevation Gain: 440 feet
High Point: 9,800 feet
Rating: Easy
Time Allowed: 1 hour
Maps: 7½ ' Engineer Mountain
San Juan National Forest

Spud Lake is a short, easy hike but a rewarding one. It is reached via U.S. Highway 550 about thirty miles north of Durango. At the bottom of Coal Bank Hill, just after crossing Cascade Creek, turn right on Lime Creek Road and go three and one-half miles to where the road passes a lily pond. Just as the road turns sharply east to go by the north side of the pond, there is a turnoff big enough to park two or three cars. The trail begins there and weaves around in basically a northerly direction. At first it is wide enough for a four-wheel-drive vehicle. At two-tenths mile, the trail moves straight ahead up a steep little rise, while the four-wheel-drive road turns left downhill. Beyond this point, the rest of the trail is easy to follow. It passes through aspen trees and, shortly before the lake, past several old beaver ponds.

The lake is officially named Potato Lake. Rising as a steep cliff out of the north side of the lake is Potato Hill. They are known popularly as Spud Lake and Spud Mountain. The lake provides several acres of good fishing. It is a lovely spot, with Spud Mountain very close on the north, the Twilight Peaks to the east across Lime Creek, and Engineer Mountain to the north-west. Engineer cannot be seen from the lake, but it can be viewed from several points along the trail. This is a beautiful hike during the summer, but it is especially beautiful during the early fall, when the aspen leaves are in full color. This is usually around October 1, but the colors are likely to be good ten days before and after this date.

Lime Creek Road is rocky in places but can be driven in a sedan if you drive carefully. The drive is lovely all the way

109

around to its north terminus at the lowest spot between Coal Bank Pass and Molas Pass on U.S. Highway 550.

Spud Lake with large beaver lodge and Spud Mountain (South side).

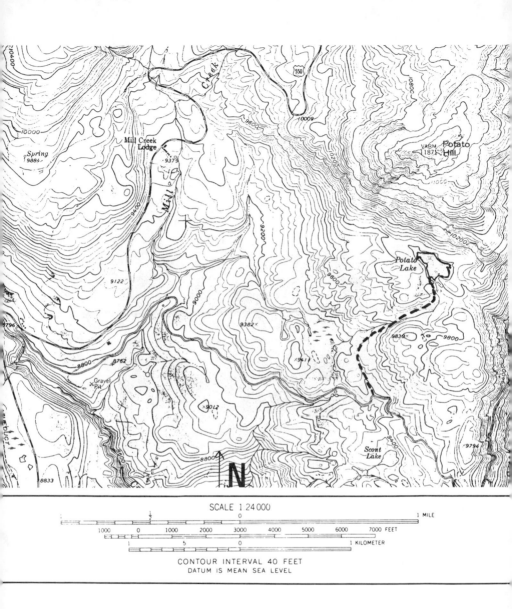

SCALE 1 24 000

CONTOUR INTERVAL 40 FEET
DATUM IS MEAN SEA LEVEL

111

Spud Mountain from northwest showing U.S. highway just below Coal
Bank Pass.

Potato Hill (Spud Mountain)

Distance: 3 miles (round trip)
Starting Elevation: 10,030 feet
Elevation Gain: 1,841 feet
High Point: 11,871 feet
Rating: Difficult
Time Allowed: 3 hours
Maps: 7½ ' Engineer Mountain
San Juan National Forest

Spud Mountain is short compared to its neighbors, Engineer Mountain to the west and the Twilight Peaks and West Needles to the east, but it stands alone and makes a good half-day hike. The view south from the top is impressive. It includes the Cascade and Animas valleys and Electra Lake far below. Purgatory Ski Area is to the southwest.

Spud Mountain is best climbed from the west or north. This is a bushwhacking route most of the way on either route through large spruce and fir. There are traces of trail near the top that other hikers and elk have used.

The west approach starts about one mile west of the peak at a hairpin turn on U.S. Highway 550, thirty-three miles north of Durango. There is adequate parking just above the hairpin turn on the west side of the road. Hikers should start eastward and aim for the rocky area just north of the top. The last several hundred yards contain some exposure and involve some interesting rock scrambling.

The north approach is about twice as long as the west route but has the advantage of starting at a higher altitude. For this route, park in the area at the top of Coal Bank Pass at 10,600 feet and strike out along the ridge toward the peak; it is basically south with a few degrees bias eastward. Again, it requires bushwhacking most of the way, with pieces of a trail available now and then. The last few hundred yards will be on rocks—the same route used from the west approach.

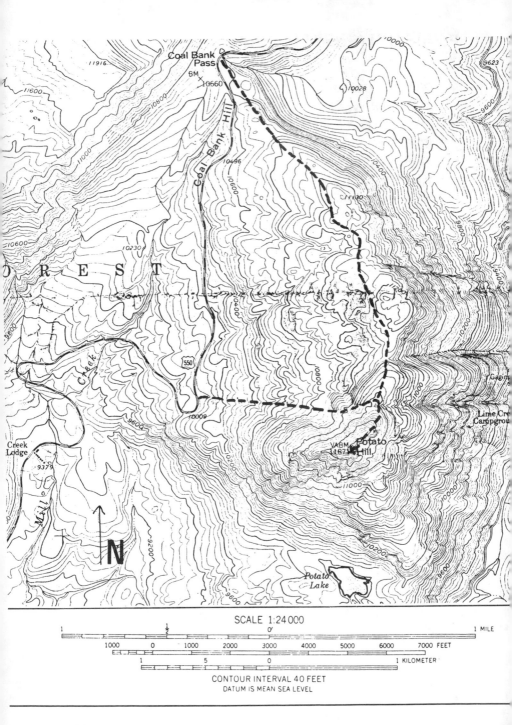

SCALE 1:24 000

CONTOUR INTERVAL 40 FEET
DATUM IS MEAN SEA LEVEL

Engineer Mountain

Distance: 4.4 miles (round trip)
Starting Elevation: 10,660 feet
Elevation Gain: 2,308 feet
High Point: 12,968 feet
Rating: Difficult
Time Allowed: 4 to 5 hours
Maps: 7½' Engineer Mountain
San Juan National Forest

Engineer Mountain is one of the most photographed peaks in the San Juans. It is reached by U.S. Highway 550 between Durango and Silverton. As you approach from Durango about ten miles south of the peak, it appears as a symmetrical cone rising straight ahead as if out of the highway. From Jarvis meadows just north of the Purgatory Ski Area turnoff, it totally dominates the northerly view.

The shortest and easiest climb begins at the top of Coal Bank Pass, where there is generous parking space. The trail starts on the west side of the road and zigzags up a steep, grassy slope northeastward into the big spruce-fir timber. Once inside the timber, it swings back gradually westward. Two lovely little lakes lie on the left side of this trail. At about one and one-half miles, the trail emerges out of the timber onto the tundra. At this point, hikers should leave the trail and head directly for the northeast ridge of the mountain. The tundra area here has many beautiful wild flowers. As you move up the beginning of the cone, the tundra rises steeply, later giving way to rock—mostly talus with a few small ledges. Take the right side of the ridge at first, then move up onto the ridge itself.

The ridge is narrow—two to four feet wide in places. Much of the rock is loose, and there is much exposure here. Therefore, you must test each handhold before trusting it. A little higher up, you emerge out on the cone itself. The top is not far beyond.

Since Engineer stands alone, even though it is a little less than 13,000 feet, the panorama of peaks and valleys to be seen is great in all directions. The north face of Engineer is a sheer drop of 800 feet. Looking down this direction, you can see a fine example of a rock glacier at the head of one of the branches of Engine Creek.

Rock glaciers are somewhat unique to the San Juan Mountains. They look like a giant pudding flowing in slow waves. In fact, they are talus rocks that do move in a very slow pattern. They are not fully understood, but the best geological theory seems to be that they are moved by ice in and under the rock.

The climbing route up the northeast ridge of Engineer Mountain rising out of the tundra.

If you have an extra couple of hours, you might want to go west from the top, over the small shoulder peak, and around to the north side and back to the tundra and trail across the rock glaciers. The west descent beyond the shoulder is over steep talus but is quite usable. Hiking the waves themselves involves some up-and-down work, all on loose rocks. You must be especially careful crossing leading edges of the waves, since the rocks are typically at the maximum angle of repose; hiking over them can start a hazardous rock slide. At several places along this area, you can hear underground streams gurgling through the rocks.

116

San Juan National Forest gives the name Engineer Mountain Trail to an approach from the south. It is more than twice as long as the Coal Bank Pass route and involves 3,920 feet of altitude gain. This is a favorite trail for elk hunters in the fall. Hikers might be interested in it as an alternate or a return route, keeping in mind that the south end of it joins U.S. Highway 550 some five miles down from Coal Bank Pass. This trail is in good condition and offers some fine views southward from several open meadows. To take it from Engineer Mountain look for it crossing north-south along the base of the east side of the cone. It soon drops down into heavy timber and goes mostly straight south four miles to a junction with U.S. Highway 550 at an electrical substation one mile above where the highway crosses Cascade Creek.

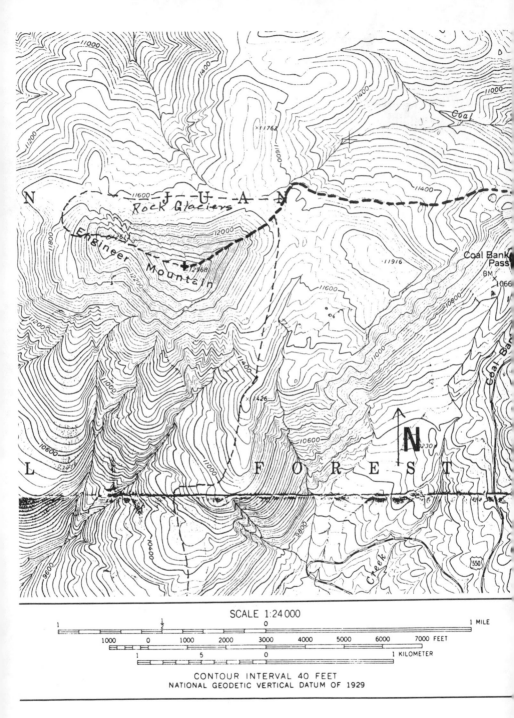

SCALE 1:24 000

CONTOUR INTERVAL 40 FEET
NATIONAL GEODETIC VERTICAL DATUM OF 1929

Grizzly Peak

Distance: 7 miles (round trip)
Starting Elevation: 11,000 feet
Elevation Gain: 2,738 feet
High Point: 13,738 feet
Rating: Difficult; hard by alternate return route
Time Allowed: 6 to 7 hours
Maps: 7½ ' Ophir
7½ ' Engineer Mountain
San Juan National Forest

Grizzly Peak is a challenging and rewarding climb. It rises out of the west side of the Cascade Creek Valley five miles northwest of Engineer Mountain. It is ten miles back from the road and can only be seen from U.S. Highway 550 thirty miles north of Durango, between the Purgatory Ski Area turnoff and the Cascade Creek crossing. As you travel northward here, you can see its peak and steep east side up the Cascade Valley to the left and beyond Engineer Mountain. It can be climbed from Cascade Valley, but this is a long route and involves two days.

The easiest route is the one described here. For this approach, turn west on the ski area turnoff twenty-eight miles north of Durango. As you approach the ski area itself, turn right (north) up a little road at the east end of the parking lot. This road soon climbs back to the west and overlooks the ski area. At the top of the climb, the road turns north and descends slightly; in about one-half mile, the main road makes a ninety-degree turn left and leads downhill to Hermosa Park. You should go straight on past this turn for approximately another mile. At this point, the road divides again; take the right turn uphill instead of the road straight ahead. You will now be moving east on a logging road that soon curves around to the north high on the shoulder of Graysill Mountain, with Cascade Creek far below and Engineer Mountain beyond to the northeast. You should go all the way to the end of the road—about eight miles. Some of this road requires a four-wheel-drive vehicle. Also, since it is a logging road, it is subject to possible cutoff by the forest service. If the road should be cut, it may still be better to hike to the end of the

Grizzly Peak; the trail goes around the base of the high foreground ridge.

road than to take another route.

At the end of the road, facing north, you will be looking down into the valley of an unnamed creek and across it to a high, rocky ridge that looks like a mountain in its own right.

Begin hiking by crossing the stream below and contouring around the southeast shoulder of the ridge at timberline. There is a partial trail here that you should find and follow. This will turn north as you round the point of the ridge. In about another mile, you will come to a delightful shelf with some small lakes and marshy areas. A stream fills this area from above, and another drains it, plunging over to the side down to Cascade Creek.

At the southwest side of this area, climb steeply upward toward the northwest. Soon you should see a steep chute of big rocks with cliffs on each side. The right side of this is a shoulder of Grizzly Peak, the top of which you cannot see from here. Climb the chute (northwest). It is somewhat tedious but better than the alternatives. At the top, you will find yourself on a rocky ridge; turn right for a fairly easy quarter-mile climb over talus to the top of the mountain. The top itself is very rocky, but it affords

An alternate route from the one described starts near Bolam Pass. (Four-wheel-drive vehicles are advisable for this route, but when the road is good, high-clearance two-wheel drives can make it; you do have to ford Hermosa Creek, which can be risky for two-wheel drives in the early summer when the creek is still swollen with snowmelt.) For this route, take the main road above Purgatory Ski Area down into Hermosa Park. At its west end, the road turns north and follows Hermosa Creek up to its head-waters. About two miles up this road after leaving Hermosa Park there is a division in the road, with the left turn going to Hotel Draw and Scotch Creek; *do not* take this turn, but go straight on. Eventually, you should come to the ghost town of Graysill, which was active in uranium mining in the 1940s and 1950s. Park here and hike northeast along the west side of the ridge leading to Grizzly. There is a trail much of the way. This route involves a very steep rocky climb up the west side of Grizzly. There is an unnamed peak a mile south of Grizzly. You will find it easier to climb over this peak from a saddle southwest of it than to climb directly up the west side of Grizzly. If you do this, you will then have to follow the tricky ridge, described above, on over to Grizzly.

The climbing chute above the lakes on Grizzly Peak.

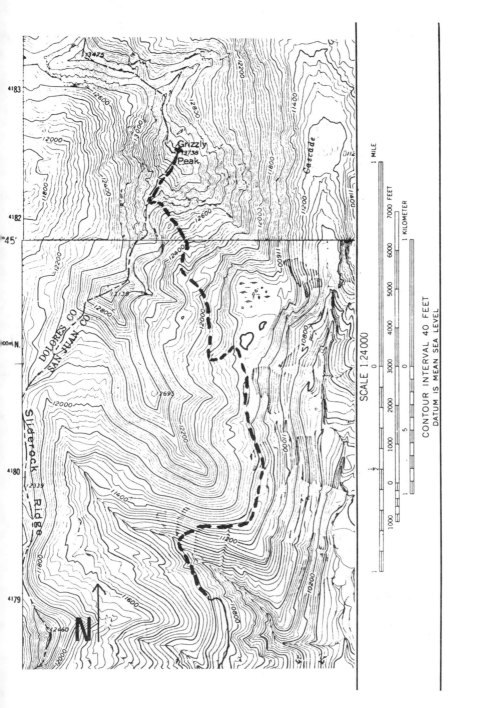

SCALE 1:24 000

CONTOUR INTERVAL 40 FEET
DATUM IS MEAN SEA LEVEL

Jura Knob (Coal Creek, Deer Creek)

Distance: 8.5 miles (loop trip)
Starting Elevation: 10,300 feet
Elevation Gain: 2,314 feet
High Point: 12,814 feet
Rating: Moderate
Time Allowed: 5 to 6 hours
Maps: 7½ Engineer Mountain
San Juan National Forest

But the objective on this hike is back eastward through Deer Creek. To do this, go back down over the shoulder-high ledge. Just below it, you can drop down the steep hillside into Deer Creek through the scree and a stretch of knee-high willows. It is easier to go back along the approach ridge further and drop down where the hillside is not so steep. Most of the Deer Creek Trail lies on the east side of the creek, although near the beginning of the creek you may find a bit of trail on the west side. Assuming that you have not found it on the west side, cross the creek, and you will find the trail a little ways beyond. The trail then follows down the creek, staying on the east side near the creek a considerable distance. There is a riot of wild flowers along this trail up to where it enters the heavily wooded area. Inside the tall timber, the trail stays high as the stream plunges rapidly downward. About a mile above the highway, the trail again emerges into a clearing and zigzags rapidly down to the highway 800 feet below, entering an aspen grove just before its finish.

Deer Creek Trail, round trip, makes a good half-day hike by itself. There is a thousand-foot climb in the first mile, but it is a good switchback trail. To find the trail head, from U.S. Highway 550: it is the second drainage north of Coal Bank Pass and the second south of Molas Pass. Just north of the creek on the east side of the highway is good parking space. About 150 yards north of the parking area, you should find the trail starting upward. Currently, there is no sign to mark it.

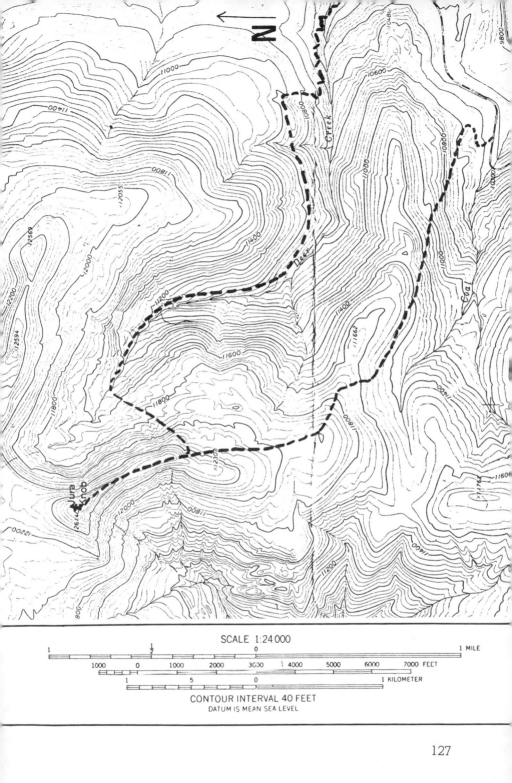

SCALE 1:24 000

1 ⊢ ½ ⊢ 0 ⊢ 1 MILE

1000 ⊢ 0 ⊢ 1000 ⊢ 2000 ⊢ 3000 ⊢ 4000 ⊢ 5000 ⊢ 6000 ⊢ 7000 FEET

1 ⊢ 5 ⊢ 0 ⊢ 1 KILOMETER

CONTOUR INTERVAL 40 FEET

DATUM IS MEAN SEA LEVEL

Sultan – Grand Turk

Distance: 7.5 miles round trip (8 miles if
  Grand Turk is included)
Starting Elevation: 10,910 feet
Elevation Gain: 2,458 feet
High Point: 13,368 feet
Rating: Difficult
Time Allowed: 5½ to 6½ hours
Maps: 7½′ Snowdon Peak
     7½′ Silverton
     San Juan National Forest

it. Climb up into the saddle and northeast over this peak. When you drop down to the next saddle (still headed northeast), you will have lost 200 feet. You are now at the base of Grand Turk.

To climb Grand Turk, add another half mile to the seven and one-half miles listed in the heading. It is fairly easy to do, however. Just continue straight up the ridge, and where it begins to level off put a bit, veer off to the right. Grand Turk has trouble deciding where to peak out. Actually, it has three peaks close to gether that are about the same height. The topographic map labels the one furthest east at 13,148 feet and does not give heights for the others. Actually, Grand Turk has twin peaks still a little further east (but these are a hundred or more feet lower than the three listed. These twin peaks are what you see of the three-peak split-topped mountain most frequently viewed from the highway and the train.

To continue on to Sultan, go back along the top of Grand Turk's ridge to a northwest descent along Turk's broad ridge. You will lose 700 feet down to the next saddle between Grand Turk and Sultan.

If you choose not to climb Grand Turk, take a cutoff to your right (east) from just west of the top in the same saddle just mentioned. This point is at 12,776 feet. Follow up the ridge northwest to the top of Sultan at 13,368 feet.

Sultan provides a fine view northeast down on Silverton, 3,600 feet below. North is Anvil Mountain which connects with Red Mountain. In the valley, U.S. Highway 550 leads on toward Ouray. To the west below is Bear Creek, and just beyond is Bear Mountain (12,987 feet). Beyond this is far, far country with many rugged peaks and ridges.

The return can be made by the same route or by an alternate. For the alternate, go west down the nose of the peak. This looks pretty steep from above, but once on it, you will find it not too bad. You soon reach a steep drainage headed southwest down the mountainside. Follow down or near this to the basin below. Since the side of the mountain is mostly talus, patience and care are called for on this descent, but it is not difficult if you do not get too far south, where it is steeper.

Once in the basin, contour around at first southwest and later more directly south. This will take you along the west side of the massif you climbed earlier. Continuing on around eventually southeast, you should be able to spot Little Molas Lake and go on down to your point of origin. Actually, if you stay a little low as you round the south end of the massif, you should strike a trail coming from the west and headed for Little Molas.

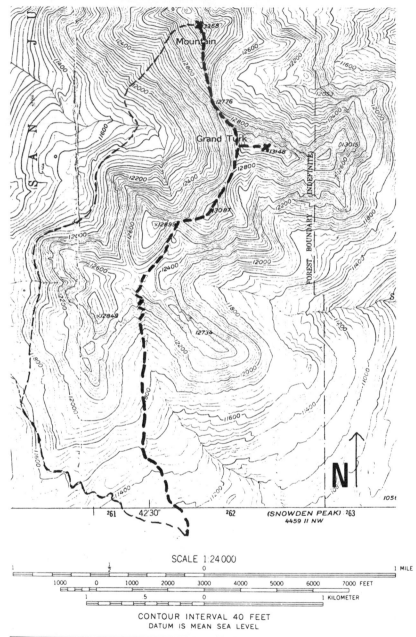

Crater Lake — Twilight Peaks

Distance: 5 miles to Crater Lake; 1.2 miles more to
North Twilight Peak; plus equal return mileage
Starting Elevation: 10,750 feet
Elevation Gain: 890 feet to Crater Lake; 1,435 feet
additional to North Twilight
High Point: 11,640 feet at Crater Lake; 13,075 feet at
North Twilight Peak
Rating: Easy but long to Crater Lake; difficult
to the peak
Time Allowed: 4 to 5 hours to Crater Lake; 2 hours
additional to North Twilight (round trip times)
Maps: 7½ ' Snowdon Peak
San Juan National Forest

This is a combination hike with two possible destinations, both of which are highly worthwhile.

The trail head is at Andrews Lake, which is reached via U.S. Highway 550 about eight miles south of Silverton. Andrews Lake is less than a mile southeast of the highway. The road to Andrews Lake turns off the highway a mile south of the summit of Molas Pass.

Park at Andrews Lake. The trail, which may be picked up on either the south or north side of the lake, moves east beyond the lake and soon turns south, zigzagging up 400 feet. After this, it continues south to Crater Lake, only rising sharply for short distances. The trail moves in and out of the edge of the timber, affording fine views northward toward the mountains surrounding Silverton and westward across Lime Creek Valley to Engineer Mountain and Grand Turk. The high spruce-fir bands of forest on both sides of this valley are excellent elk hunting areas.

The last clearing where the trail turns east for a half mile affords a distinctive view of the steep north face of the Twilight massif. About a mile beyond this, you reach the lake, a lovely little high-altitude gem surrounded by tall trees; timberline is just above it.

Twilight West Needles massif from the open meadow ascent of Larch Knob.

The hike into the lake and back can be done in a long half day. Some may want to take advantage of the excellent camping sites here and perhaps do a little fishing and relaxing. The hike to Crater Lake and back is rated fairly easy, but long.

For those who would like to climb Twilight, the challenge has just begun, for the next mile brings steep climbing and one and a half times as much altitude gain as has already been made in five miles.

To begin the ascent, follow around the north side of the lake, and start the climb eastward beyond the lake. There is no fixed trail beyond this point, but you should have no difficulty finding your way because you are out of the timber by this time. A few hundred yards southeast and 150 feet higher is another little lake. At this point, turn southwest, and ascend steeply toward the peak. The first top is a false one; from it you must climb down a little. Be careful here, for there is considerable exposure in this little dip. Climb out of the dip to the top a quarter mile beyond. The top itself is a smooth roll.

132

From the top, you can see to the east the rugged Needles territory where there are three 14,000-foot mountains as well as a myriad of other steep and rugged peaks. This is truly wilderness, roadless territory. Between Twilight and the Needles steeply below is the Animas River valley. If you are there at the right time of day, you might even hear the little Durango-Silverton train whistle its loneliness up out of the valley.

North Twilight is a part of a massif called the West Needle Mountains; this includes Snowdon Peak to the north and Twilight, South Twilight, and West Needle Mountain to the south. All of these peaks are in the 13,000-foot class. Hikers who have time and energy left after reaching North Twilight could take in Twilight and South Twilight in the next mile. The drop between North Twilight and Twilight is only about 400 feet. Twilight Peak (the middle of the Twilights) is actually the highest of the group at 13,158 feet.

The return trip is ordinarily made by the same route as the approach.

Hikers who like steep climbing might want to try bushwhacking directly up the west side of this massif instead of taking the long hike from Andrews Lake. This route would involve taking Lime Creek Road off U.S. Highway 550. At about the midpoint of this ride loop there is a parking and picnic area, formerly maintained as a campground by the forest service. Lime Creek is a good-sized stream, usually with a complement of fishermen and picnickers. There is no trail on this route. It is only for the hardy. First you must wade the stream, fight your way through a short band of tangled brush, then move steeply upward. Twilight and North Twilight are only a little over a mile above the creek, but more than 4,000 feet of altitude must be gained in this distance. A drainage comes down between these two peaks with a nice little lake just below the peaks well above timberline. This route is rated very difficult.

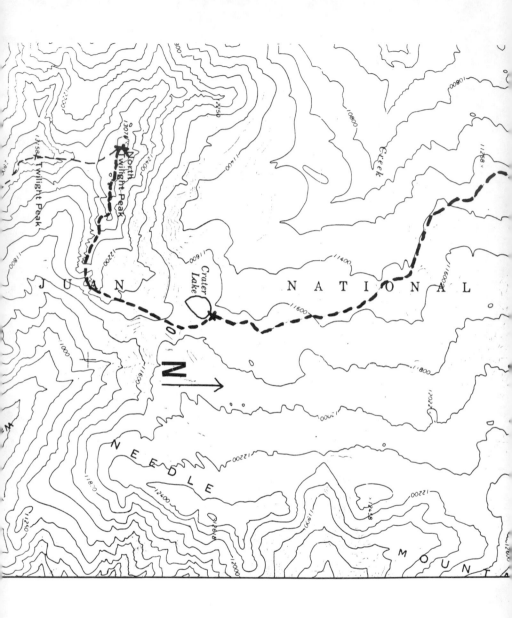

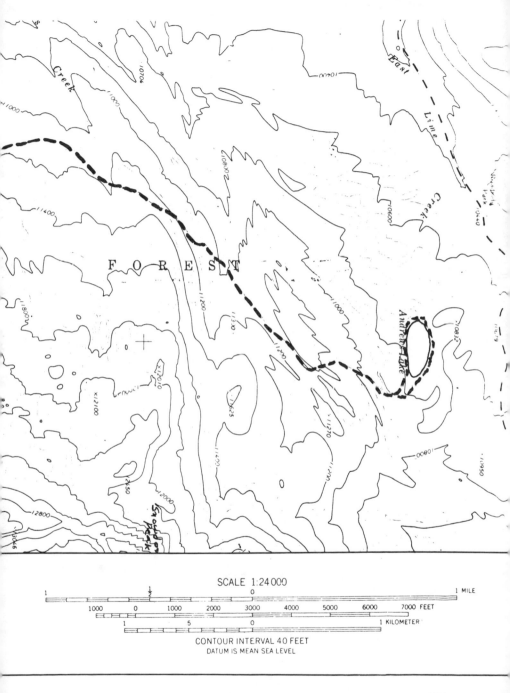

SCALE 1:24 000

1 ········ ½ ········ 0 ·· 1 MILE

1000 ···· 0 ···· 1000 ·· 2000 ·· 3000 ·· 4000 ·· 5000 ·· 6000 ·· 7000 FEET

1 ···· 5 ···· 0 ·········· 1 KILOMETER

CONTOUR INTERVAL 40 FEET
DATUM IS MEAN SEA LEVEL

Twilight-West Needles from Spud Lake.

Snowdon Peak

Distance: 6 miles (round trip)
Starting Elevation: 10,744 feet
Elevation Gain: 2,333 feet
High Point: 13,077 feet
Rating: Hard
Time Allowed: 5 hours
Maps: 7½ : Snowdon Peak
San Juan National Forest

Snowdon is a twin-peaked mountain with each peak sloping gently toward the low point between. The two are quite symmetrical and make a distinctive skyline view eastward from U.S. Highway 550 as you travel toward the top of Molas Pass from the south. Though the two peaks slope gently toward each other in a north-south direction, the view you get from the west side makes the climb look impossible. It is a steep slab 800 feet down from the top. Though this is not the route suggested here, the climb should still be rated hard.

The approach is the same as for Crater Lake-Twilight. Take the Andrews Lake road one mile south of Molas Pass. Park at the lake, and hike east along either side of the lake. Turning south, you will find the trail zigzagging up a 400-foot rise; just beyond the top of this hill, you will find two little lakes below you on your left. Here you must leave the trail; the rest of the hike will require bushwhacking except for a few short pieces of trail. Turn east between these two lakes. (At some times of the year they may be little more than swamps.) Cross a half mile of flats, then a slowly rising area. There is a smaller peak to the north of the most northerly of the Snowdon peaks. Contour upward through the timber toward this peak and, above timberline, a bit to the right to strike the saddle between this peak and the north Snowdon peak. Continue up this ridge, now hiking south toward the top of Snowdon. Within a few hundred yards of the top, the rocks become difficult on the face of the ridge. Here you should go a bit to the east side of the ridge and climb south, finishing up ...

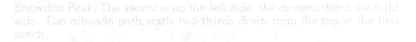

Snowdon Peak. The ascent is up the left side; the descent down the right side. The glissade path starts two thirds down from the top at the first notch.

137

the summit. There is substantial exposure in this last section. All handholds and footholds should be carefully tested before being trusted. Climbers may need to stay close together to help each other through this area. Rope could be used here, but most experienced climbers do not rope up for this short distance. The top itself widens out to a broad roll of small rocks. It is fairly large.

The views from the top include the Animas Valley steeply below to the east and the dramatic Grenadier Range straight east beyond. Mount Garfield is the first peak in the range. The Grenadiers are a favorite place for technical climbers. Straight north is Grand Turk on the west side of the highway and Sultan Mountain beyond. Just east of Sultan, on the right side of the valley, is Kendall Mountain, which is the peak that towers over the east side of Silverton. Beyond these is a grand panorama of many peaks.

Of the twin Snowdon peaks, the north one, which is the approach route described here, is the higher.

The return may be varied from the approach. Go south toward the low point between the two peaks. There is a break in the rock here, and you will have to do some rock scrambling to get down. At the bottom of this scramble you are faced with some interesting rock pylons. To the right is a steep couloir that can be used with care. Sometimes there is enough snow here for a good glissade, but the slope is steep, and ice axes are advisable for a possible arrest. A more gradual route down can be found by keeping to the left. Either route circles from west to north. At the bottom of this steep area (now 1,000 feet below the north peak), continue north or a little northwest to get back to the flat swampy area from which the approach was made. Westward across this will bring you back to the Crater Lake Trail again. Turn right on it to go back to Andrews Lake.

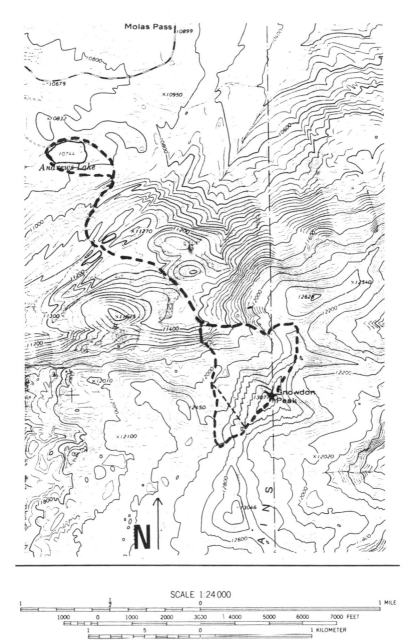

Molas Pass /10899
×10950
Andrews Lake
Snowdon Peak

SCALE 1:24 000

CONTOUR INTERVAL 40 FEET
DATUM IS MEAN SEA LEVEL

Graysill Mountain — Grayrock Peak

Distance: 6.3 miles (round trip)
Starting Elevation: 10,300 feet
Elevation Gain: 2,504 feet
High Point: 12,504 feet
Rating: Moderate
Time Allowed: 3 ½ to 4 ½ hours
Maps: 7 ½ ' Engineer Mountain
     San Juan National Forest

Graysill Mountain is a formation in the shape of a horseshoe facing east; it peaks out on its southeast corner, and at that point it is called Grayrock Peak. It is not a high peak compared to many of the others in the San Juans, but since it is the highest point for several miles in any direction, it is impressive and yields fine views. It is located west of Cascade Creek and southwest of Engineer Mountain.

Graysill lies north of Purgatory Ski Area. To reach it, take U.S. Highway 550 twenty-eight miles north of Durango, and turn left (west) on the ski area road. As you approach the ski area itself, turn right (north) up a little road at the east end of the ski parking lot. This road climbs in a series of switchbacks to the top of the ski slope. Here it turns north. In a half mile there is a left turn down into Hermosa Park; do not take this, but go on for about a mile, and turn right (east) uphill. Follow this road four and one-half miles. It swings eastward to the shoulder of Cascade Creek Canyon, and then turns to the north. You eventually pass along the east shoulder of Graysill and can look up to your destination sharply above. The four and one-half miles bring you beyond Grayrock Peak to Pando Creek. Park in any wide spot near the creek. Three branches of Pando come together near the place where the road crosses the creek.

Start the hike west along the most northerly branch of the creek. The northern point of the horseshoe will be ahead and to your right. There is no trail here; bushwhacking is required, but it should not be too difficult. If you stay a bit to the right of the creek, you get out of the timber in a half mile; if you stay near the stream, the timber carries on for a mile. At any rate, aim for a shallow saddle at the top of the drainage. Once here, you will find a relatively flat tundra area. To reach the peak, swing left for an easy 1.8 miles to the top. The saddle is nearly 800 feet below the peak, but the climb is gradual and therefore not difficult. The route goes south from the saddle and gradually curves more eastward, ending up almost straight east.

Grayrock Peak features its own special thrill—a sheer cliff on its north side, practically straight down for a thousand feet. After recovering from the sight of this glimpse, you will want to enjoy the more distant views. Engineer rises as a lone, stalwart warrior out of Cascade Canyon 3.8 miles northeast. Grizzly is a sharp and dominant point six miles north, even higher than Engineer. Eastward are the West Needles and the Twilight peaks. Northwest are Hazelton Peak and the Bolam Pass area. On the southwest skyline are the La Plata Mountains.

The return should be made by the same route as the climb. You could cut down to the road and back to the parking spot to maneuver a mile by following the northbound ridge, but some of this is very steep, much of it as told us.

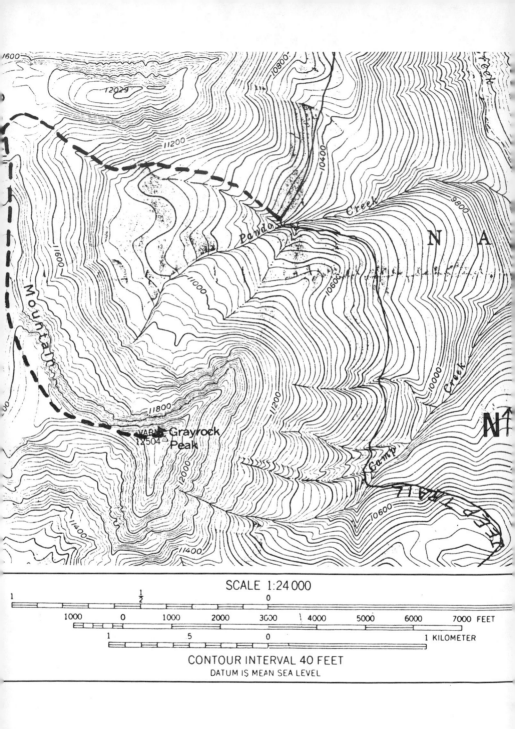

SCALE 1:24 000

CONTOUR INTERVAL 40 FEET
DATUM IS MEAN SEA LEVEL

Hermosa Peak

Distance: 1.5 miles (round trip)
Starting Elevation: 11,520 feet
Elevation Gain: 1,059 feet
High Point: 12,579 feet
Rating: Moderate
Time Allowed: 1½ to 2½ hours
Maps: 7½' Hermosa Peak
San Juan National Forest

Hermosa Peak involves traveling some backcountry roads, but once there, it is one of the easiest and quickest high-altitude climbs in southwestern Colorado. It offers fine views of even higher peaks from its top; even driving the road to it is a worthwhile experience. The climb is quite short but is rated moderate because it is high and because some 250 yards of it are steep, though not very hazardous.

Access is via the Bolam Pass four-wheel-drive road. This road, however, is usually in better condition than many such roads. Under dry conditions, two-wheel-drive cars and trucks can usually make it if they have good clearance and a good low gear for the steep hills. This road may be approached from the east or the west. For the eastern approach, take U.S. Highway 550 twenty-eight miles north of Durango to the Purgatory Ski Area turnoff; go west on it to the Purgatory parking area. At the east end of the parking lot, take a right (north) turn up a gravel road. This leads up above Purgatory and furnishes fine views of the ski runs, the valley below, and the West Needles–Twilight massif east across Lime Creek. This is especially spectacular during the fall foliage color season (the end of September and early October). At the top of the ridge above Purgatory, this road turns north; four-tenths mile beyond this, take the first left down into Hermosa Park. This is a lovely valley surrounded by aspen- and spruce-covered mountains. At the west end of the park, the road turns north and follows closely beside Hermosa Creek. This is a good-sized stream and must be forded a mile above the park. Except during the high water of spring snowmelt, the fording should be no problem even for two-wheel-drive

143

cars if you approach it resolutely and do not try to cross too slowly.

Six miles beyond the ford and 1,900 feet higher you come to a little open shelf and the mining ghost town of Graysill. It is in better condition than some abandoned mining towns because it was involved in uranium and vanadium mining. This puts it into a later period of history. It is worth a stop here for a view and a picture back down Hermosa Valley. One and four-tenths miles further brings you to the top of Bolam Pass at 11,400 feet. Here again you get a good view. To the north and a little east is Grizzly Peak, just short of 14,000 feet. To the northwest, and look across Lizard Head Pass to Lizard Head Peak and the San Miguel massif, which contains three fourteeners. Wilson Peak, Mount Wilson, and El Diente.

Seven-tenths mile beyond Bolam Pass, you make a sharp little dip down to cross over a culvert carrying a small stream. Just beyond this, the main road turns right; but to go to Hermosa Peak, which dominates the southern skyline, turn left. This road starts southeast but soon turns southwest across an open, flat meadow. Follow the road to the west side of the mountain. It crosses some talus at the base of the peak. Here it is not much over a quarter mile, in a straight line, to the top, but you should drive on another .2 to .3 mile and park off the road.

It is eighteen miles from U.S. Highway 550 at the Purgatory turnoff to the point where the Hermosa Peak Road separates off from the Bolam Pass Road.

Access from the west route is via Colorado State Highway 145. On this side, the road is called Barlow Creek Road, but it is the same road as Bolam Pass Road. It turns east off Highway 145, six miles north of Rico or six miles south of Lizard Head Pass. Just across the Dolores River, a very nice forest service campground is located north of the road along the river. Barlow Creek Road turns right, whereas the road straight ahead goes off into the campground. It is seven miles and 1,800 feet of rise on up to the route that turns off to Hermosa Peak. This junction is in an open space in a flat area, so it should not be hard to find. From there on, follow the directions given above to reach the peak.

The climb starts out east up an easy, grassy slope. (There may be a few trees at first, depending on your choice of a parking spot.) The grassy slope heads toward a saddle south of the peak. This is quite easy climbing except just below the saddle, where it gets steeper and becomes talus.

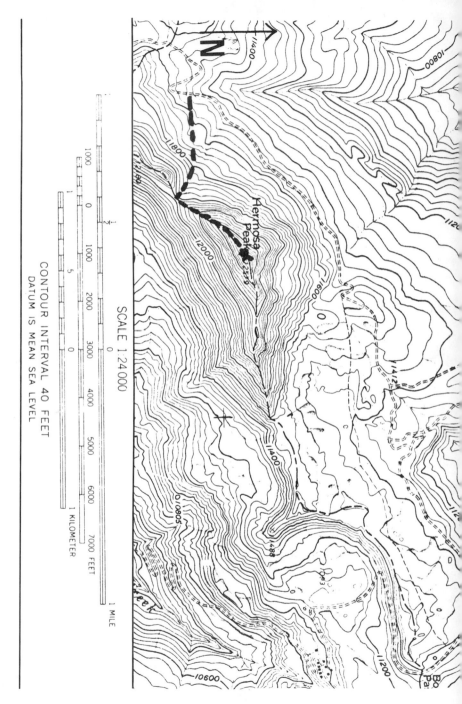

SCALE 1:24 000

CONTOUR INTERVAL 40 FEET
DATUM IS MEAN SEA LEVEL

CHAPTER 6

Hikes Out of Silverton

South Mineral Creek — Cascade

Distance: 8.8 miles (one way)
Starting Elevation: 10,680 feet
Elevation Gain: 1,800 feet
High Point: 12,480 feet
Rating: Moderate, but fairly long
Time Allowed: 5 to 7 hours
Maps: 7½ ' Ophir
7½ ' Engineer Mountain
San Juan National Forest

This is a hike that is highly rewarding in beauty without re-
quiring any difficult climbing. The beauty is in the natural
scenery of nearby peaks and in a large expanse of wild flowers.
Some people use this route for backpacking and an overnight
stay, but it certainly can be done in a day, including time to
enjoy the scenery and take pictures. It is a hike that does not
return to the starting point; you will need someone to take you to
the starting point and pick you up at the other end. A four-wheel
drive is best, but in dry weather, a vehicle with good clearance
can make it.

147

The launching point is South Mineral Campground. The road to the campground turns off U.S. Highway 550 two miles northwest of Silverton. It turns sharply downhill off the south side of the highway. Five miles down the road is the lovely camp ground in tall timber next to the stream, a very nice place to spend the night if you wish to start early the next morning. Four-wheel drive and high-clearance vehicles can take hikers another two and one-half miles over a very rough road. (If you start hiking from the campground, you must add two and one-half miles and an hour to the distance and time given above.) The road goes west around the campground area turns southwest up a steep, rocky grade. It soon rises above timberline and continues on past the Bandora Mine one-half mile, where it ends at an old cabin.

The hike goes south here, veering into the forest for one-half mile before reaching and maintaining a higher level above the woods. This trail is called Rico-Silverton; farther along it becomes the Highline Trail.

Above the timber, you enter a three level spot called South Park, some of this is marshy. The wild flowers begin here with lovely marsh flowers and continue for a mile and a half up to the top of the basin at the pass, changing species with the altitude. This area can hardly be surpassed for natural floral beauty. But that is not all, for you pass Rolling Mountain (12,683 feet) on the right and the Twin Sisters (13,432 feet) and 13,374 feet rise up on the left. At the top of the pass, an unnamed peak rises less than 100 feet above the trail. If you have plenty of time, it is worth a side trip up here to get a more spectacular view.

Next a mental southeast, is Jura Knob. Several miles beyond that on the horizon are Twilight and the West Needles. Straight south is Engineer Mountain; from this side, it is a dramatic cliff plunging 200 feet, not the quintessential cone so often seen from the south side. To the southwest lies Grizzle, thrusting its ragged points skyward out of Cascade Valley somewhere.

South of the pass you continue for another mile and a half above timberline. Here the trail becomes a talus slope, but you should be able to get through this without much trouble if you contour around. Generally south, toward a north-south saddle between the peaks you have just climbed and the next one just surveyed. Stay on the west side of the saddle and traverse the steep hillside, staying at about the same level. Around the south

Looking down toward the pass which separates South Mineral Creek from
[...] Creek. Bottino Mountain rises to the right and Twin Sisters to
the [...]

[...] of this peak, you should pick up the trail again a little before
it dips back into the timber.

Before into the timber, the trail passes under a spring with water
[...] a dribbling water. A short distance further there is a narrow
creek in the trees at a little level spot. Imagine here a very
powerful view of Engineer Mountain across the way here. Engine
Creek flashes down steeply, all this is a beautiful timber, and
rushes up into the rocky grandeur. The last time I was in the area,
we camped overnight in the level spot, when the sun went down,
the moon shone brightly over Engineer, even letting this perfect
outcrop I thought. "There is nowhere else in the world I would
rather be right now."

Up to this point, the route has remained high, well beyond
here, the trail descends sharply — 1,800 feet in 1.4 miles to Cascade Creek to a little open flat where Engine Creek joins
Cascade. This is a nice spot, good for relaxing and enjoying Cascade Creek as it works its way loudly through the rocks. You
might even be able to catch a trout here.

Just a few yards upstream, the Highline Trail crosses the creek and heads west; instead of following it, pick up the Cascade Creek Trail and head downstream. In just a short distance you cross Engine Creek on a good forest service bridge. Just above the bridge, Engine Creek has a beautiful waterfall, well worth exploring and photographing. In early June, before the snow has melted enough for this full hike, it is worth hiking up to the waterfall from the south end just to see the falls. Engine Creek at this time is a raging torrent pouring tons of water over the falls every minute.

If your transportation has come up the Cascade Creek road 1.5 miles from the highway, as it should, you will have a pleasant 2.4 miles more to hike down the trail from the falls. This is not steep; it leads along Cascade Creek, mostly in big timber, but with a few open spots and wild flowers. This is a lovely hike in its own right.

Rolling Mountain from South Park.

Engine Creek Falls seen from Cascade Trail.

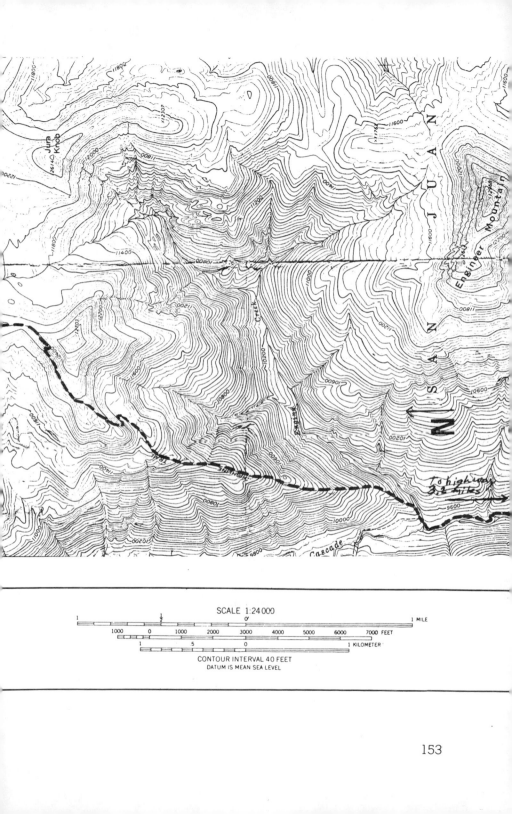

SCALE 1:24 000

CONTOUR INTERVAL 40 FEET
DATUM IS MEAN SEA LEVEL

Lake Hope

Distance: 5.3 miles (round trip)
Starting Elevation: 9,900 feet
Elevation Gain: 1,980 feet
High Point: 11,880 feet
Rating: Easy
Time Allowed: 3 hours
Maps: 7½' Ophir
        Uncompahgre National Forest

Lake Hope lies at the center of its own high basin a little above timberline. It is surrounded by dramatic, sharp peaks well above 13,000 feet. There is a breathtaking ruggedness. Some of the peaks are very colorful, with a mixture of reds, oranges, and grays. The lake can at times provide good fishing. It is reachable by a well-maintained national forest trail. It is rated easy, though the last half mile is a bit steep.

An interesting aspect of this lake is that it is a part of the water supply for the Ames power plant. Lake Hope is at the headwaters of the Lake Fork of the San Miguel River. Its water flows into Trout Lake. The varying demands of water for power can make Lake Hope beautiful when full and less attractive when drained down. This can also affect the fishing.

From Trout Lake, the water passes through a flume to the power plant. Ames is where the first commercial alternating current in the United States was generated. The motivation here was getting power more conveniently to the high-altitude mines in the area. It was difficult in the last century to get steam boilers and other heavy steam equipment up into this rugged high country. Another problem for the mine operators who used steam was fuel. Many mines were located well above timberline, so hauling wood for firing the boilers was an uphill, expensive job. Some of the mines were in danger of being shut down because of this cost.

Direct current electricity was no answer either because of the difficulty in transmitting over anything but short distances. The pioneers hit upon the idea of alternating current for ease of transmission and low losses in power. Its voltage could be easily

154

raised for long-distance transmission and again easily lowered for use. Building a power line over a mountain was much easier than hauling heavy equipment where roads were inadequate, at best. There were many doubters, but the Ames plant was put into operation in 1892 and ran successfully for thirty days without a shutdown.

The route to Lake Hope is via Highway 145. Trout Lake is on the east side of the highway just north of Lizard Head Pass between Telluride and Rico. This is about twelve miles south of the Telluride turnoff from Highway 145. At Trout Lake there is a good gravel road quite adequate for regular cars along the north side of the lake. Take it, and climb to its most southeasterly point (just under two miles from the highway). Here is a well-marked trail head and adequate parking. The road switches back to the northwest and goes on.

The trail passes through some open space, then a half mile of timber, and finally above timberline to the lake.

Lake Hope can also be approached from the east side. For this route, go two miles northwest of Silverton on U.S. Highway 550, and turn left downhill on South Mineral Creek Road. The South Mineral Campground is located six miles down this road. A four-wheel-drive vehicle is required beyond the campground. Follow the road around the campground southwest about two and one-half miles to the Bandora Mine. There are interesting beaver ponds in the course of the creek both before and beyond the campground.

The Ophir quad map shows two trails up to Lake Hope through a canyon on the north side of Rolling Mountain. The lower one starts out bravely enough but soon dissipates in the woods. The other one, however, is a good trail; in fact, it is an old road nearly all the way to the top of the pass. The first part can be traveled by four-wheel drive, but it is not worth it, for part of the road has slid away not far up.

The plan, then, is to park just below the Bandora Mine in the flat meadows off the road. Start hiking uphill on the old road on the southwest side of the mine. This route is not maintained and is rocky in places, but it is easy to follow and not too steep. It goes all the way to the top of the pass at 12,445 feet and then down the other side seven-tenths of a mile and 565 feet to the lake. The view at the top of the pass is dramatic as you first glimpse the sharp peaks, Lake Hope below, and Trout Lake still further down.

This route is three miles long one way. It starts at 10,784 feet, rises to 12,445 feet, and drops 565 feet. Total altitude gain for the round trip is 2,226 feet. This route should be rated easy except for the four-wheel-drive approach and the high altitude, which changes it to moderate.

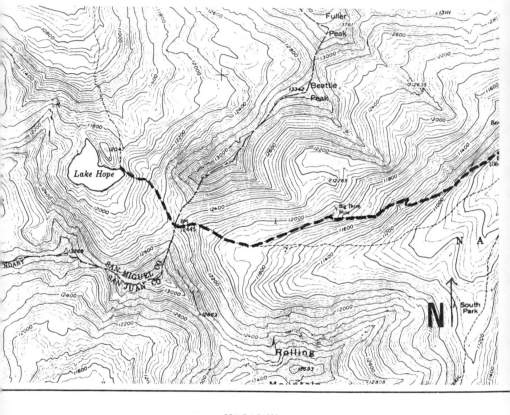

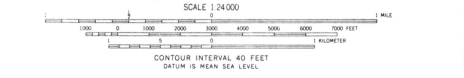

SCALE 1:24000

CONTOUR INTERVAL 40 FEET
DATUM IS MEAN SEA LEVEL

Ice Lakes

Distance: 7 miles (round trip)
Starting Elevation: 9,850 feet
Elevation Gain: 2,407 feet
High Point: 12,257 feet
Rating: Moderate
Time Allowed: 4 to 5 hours
Maps: 7½ ' Ophir
San Juan National Forest

There are two Ice Lake basins—upper and lower. The upper (main) basin is far more interesting. The lower basin in on the way to the upper; its lake is small and shallow. The main basin lies above 12,000 feet and is one of the most interesting high-altitude basins in the San Juans. There are two rather large lakes (several acres each) and several small ones. Ice Lake is at 12,257 feet. Three-quarters mile south of it at 12,585 feet is Fuller Lake. About the same distance northeast of Ice Lake on a traverse around the end of a ridge in its own basin is Island Lake. This whole basin area is surrounded by sharp and colorful peaks, all well above 13,000 feet but none quite reaching 14,000 feet.

I will only describe the hike to the basin. The peaks all make interesting climbs, but climbers can find their own routes out of the basin rather easily, for this is all open country well above timberline. These peaks, in order from south around west to north are: Fuller Peak (13,761 feet), Vermillion Peak (13,894 feet), Golden Horn (13,600 feet), Pilot Knob (13,738 feet), and U. S. Grant Peak (13,767 feet). Clear Lake, even larger than those named, is only a mile northeast of Island Lake and at a slightly lower altitude, but a high ridge separates it off. Therefore, it is to be approached by a different route.

To get to the trail head for Ice Lakes, take U.S. Highway 550 two miles northwest of Silverton. Make a left turn downhill into the valley, and drive six miles to the lovely South Mineral Campground. Park here; hike on up the road to the point where it turns south and crosses a stream. Just a few yards before this point, the Ice Lakes Trail climbs steeply up the hill (north and west). Later, it moves more westerly, climbing steadily through both straight

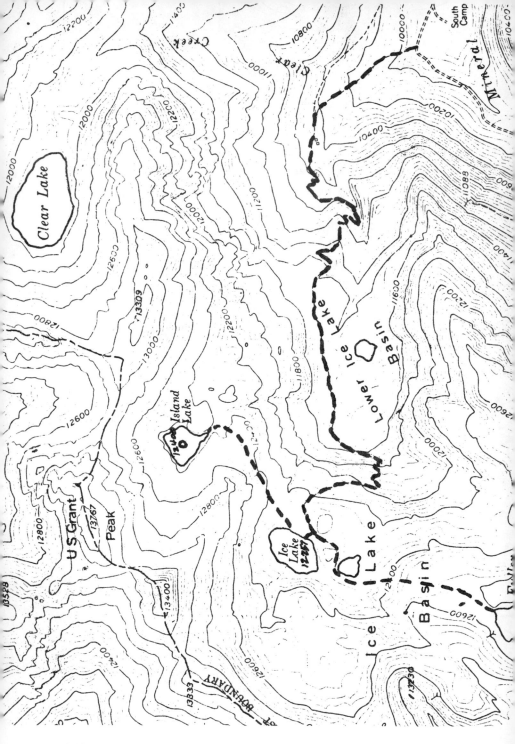

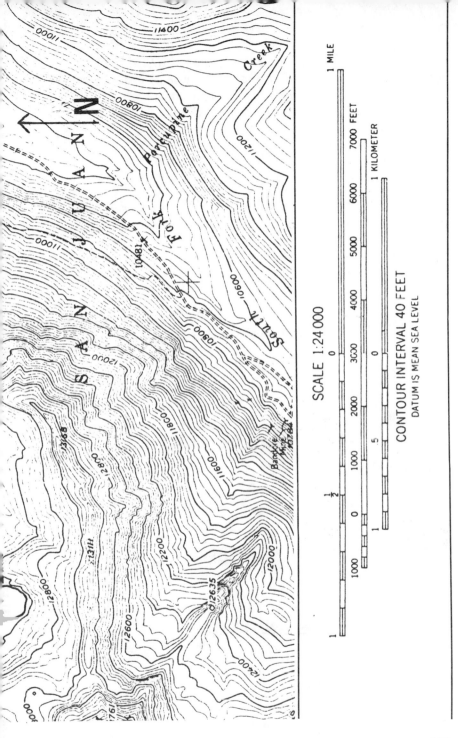

SCALE 1:24 000

CONTOUR INTERVAL 40 FEET
DATUM IS MEAN SEA LEVEL

stretches and switchbacks up to the lower basin. The trail does not climb much through the lower basin; in fact, it descends a bit. At the far end of the basin, it begins to climb again; the first two hundred yards are rocky and furnish the only difficulty in the whole trail, but it is only bad in one short spot. Another mile brings you to beautiful Ice Lake.

This is an easy trail to follow into the large, upper basin, where it quits; then you are on your own to explore the lakes and the surrounding guardian peaks. You cannot see out except to the east through South Mineral Creek Valley. But the surrounding peaks and the lakes make the hike well worthwhile. These lakes are high but large enough for good fishing. There are many beautiful wild flowers along the route and small tundra flowers in the basin itself.

The return is to be made by the same route as the approach.

ISLAND LAKE

A short and worthwhile extension of the Ice Lake trip is Island Lake. Fuller Lake is in the same basin as Ice Lake, but Island Lake is separated off in its own basin and needs some additional explanation. It is six-tenths mile farther and, at 12,400 feet, is 143 feet higher than Ice Lake. It is located in a tight

Opposite and above: Two views of Ice Lake.

glacial pocket surrounded by U. S. Grant Peak and its shoulder ridges. There is a single large, flat-topped rock island rising out of the middle of it.

To get to Island Lake, hike northeast, starting on the north side of the stream that drains Ice Lake. At first there is no trail, but looking ahead a little in the tundra you can see several sheep trails converging. From this point on, there is a well-defined trail the rest of the way around an east-west ridge to the lake. The trail has a couple of rocky spots, but the hike can be completed easily in twenty minutes. Ice Lake is frequented by many on nice weekend summer days, but Island Lake is more isolated and is seen by a much smaller number of people. It is beautiful and well worth the extra time.

U. S. GRANT PEAK

Those who wish to consider climbing U. S. Grant Peak will want to come around to Island Lake and climb along its south side to a saddle between Grant and an unnamed peak to the south. All the tops in this area are very rugged. Grant rises 1,367 feet above the lake.

Clear Lake

Distance: 7.5 miles (round trip)
Starting Elevation: 9,850 feet
Elevation Gain: 2,110 feet
High Point: 11,960 feet
Rating: Moderate
Time Allowed: 4½ to 5½ hours
Maps: 7½' Ophir
      San Juan National Forest

Clear Lake also lies above South Mineral Campground in a high-walled, tightly shaped glacial cirque. The peaks rise abruptly to over 13,000 feet right out of the lake on two sides. The north and east sides leave enough room for camping and picnicking, but the total effect on the hiker is that of being in a big, rocky pocket.

The lake itself is four-tenths mile long and about half that wide. It is a good fishing spot, but, being well above timberline, its surroundings show a harsh and rugged beauty.

There is currently an active mine high on the talus above the south side of the lake. Because of the mine, you can drive all the way to the lake on a well-maintained four-wheel-drive road, which is good enough for two-wheel-drive vehicles with high clearance when it is dry.

For hiking, you can go all the way on the road beginning two-thirds of a mile down the road toward the highway from South Mineral Campground. A more interesting route for hiking starts at the northwest corner of the campground. The Ice Lake and Clear Lake trails are one and the same for seven-tenths mile, where the Ice Lake Trail switches back left. The Clear Lake Trail goes straight on, crossing Clear Creek at a very nice falls. A couple of hundred yards farther, the trail joins the road and uses it the rest of the way to the top, two and three-fourths miles.

South Mineral Creek Valley is surrounded by steep walls and rugged, jagged peaks. Many breathtaking views appear along this route; it is well worth hiking in spite of the road.

Golden Horn from Clear Lake trail.

Clear Lake.

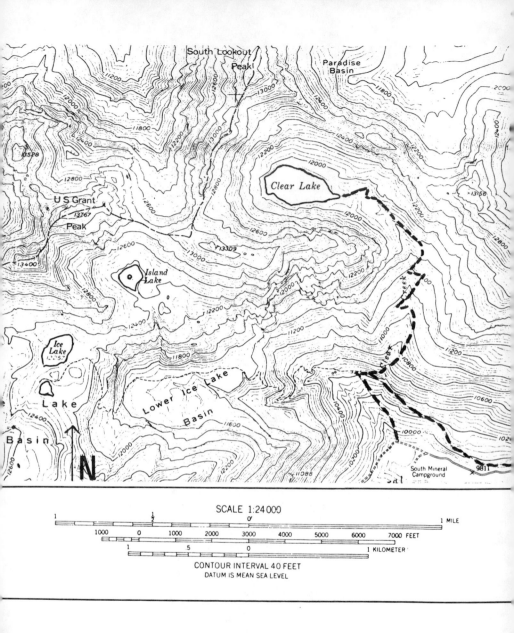

SCALE 1:24 000

CONTOUR INTERVAL 40 FEET
DATUM IS MEAN SEA LEVEL

164

Kendall Mountain

Distance: 12 miles (round trip)
Starting Elevation: 9,300 feet
Elevation Gain: 3,766 feet
High Point: 13,066 feet
Rating: Moderate
Time Allowed: 6 to 7 hours
Maps: 7½ ' Silverton
        San Juan National Forest

Kendall Mountain is just over 13,000 feet and is located directly east of Silverton. The hike described here is up a steep, rocky road. Four-wheel-drive vehicles can go most of the way to the top. Two-wheel drives can go halfway or more so that the total length of the hike can be reduced substantially if you choose to do so.

Kendall Mountain, over this same route, is the site of an annual footrace each summer. If you hike it, you see that it has to be grueling for a race. The best runners make the round trip in under two hours.

The main street in Silverton is Greene Street. Three blocks north of the south end of it, turn right and follow this street to a bridge across the Animas River. Park on either side of the bridge in a convenient spot, and start hiking south along the base of the mountain. The road spirals around and up the mountain, at first south, then southeast, east, and finally north to the top. Most of the route is open so that many fine views are accessible along most of the way. At four miles, turn left (north) toward the peak. The main road goes on up Kendall Gulch to several old mines. Near the top, the road quits, and you have to finish the climb over talus; it is only a hundred yards or so.

The return should be over the same route.

Looking down on Silverton from the top of Kendall Mountain.

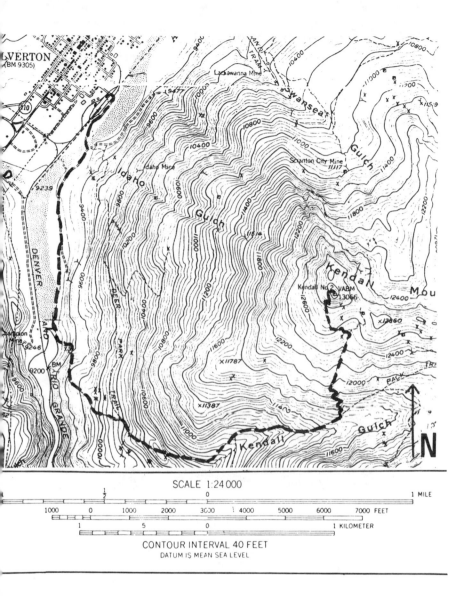

SCALE 1:24 000

CONTOUR INTERVAL 40 FEET
DATUM IS MEAN SEA LEVEL

Deer Park Trail — Whitehead Peak

Distance: 13.2 miles (round trip)
Starting Elevation: 9,300 feet
Elevation Gain: 3,959 feet
High Point: 13,259 feet
Rating: Difficult (due to length and altitude)
Time Allowed: 6 to 8 hours
Maps: 7½ ' Silverton
7½ ' Howardsville
San Juan National Forest

This hike includes a lovely high-altitude basin at timberline and a peak with good views. It lies southeast of Silverton off the Kendall Mountain Road. (See the Kendall Mountain hike on how to start up this road.) The hike distance and elevation gain are calculated from the bridge over the Animas River at Silverton. This can be shortened a great deal by those who want to drive part way. Four-wheel-drive vehicles can go all the way to the basin, cutting the round-trip hike by 6.3 miles and 1,620 feet of elevation. Two-wheel drives can cut off four or more miles.

To start the hike, take the Kendall Mountain road up 2.3 miles from the river bridge to a right turn on a smaller road; it is an easy, pleasant mile beyond this to the basin.

At the head of the basin (east) is a saddle between two high points. The one on the right is Whitehead Peak. In the basin there are several trails. To climb Whitehead, aim for the saddle, but start out at the lower end of the basin, following a little jeep road on the left (north) side that runs along the flat near the stream for most of a mile before climbing left uphill to a little plateau. The trail can be lost easily at the turnoff, for the road leads across the stream to an old cabin on the south side of the basin. The correct trail stays on the north side; from the plateau, it moves east and eventually southeast, then mounts the steep part to the top of the saddle through a series of switchbacks. Some of the trail is faint in this area. Whitehead Peak is a large rolling top a few hundred yards to the south of the saddle.

From the top there is a good view south to the Grenadiers. The view to the east down across the tundra includes the High-

The Grenadier Range from Whitehead Peak.

land Mary lakes. In fact, the trail leads on across the saddle down to these lakes in open tundra in just over two miles. You could go there and north down the Highland Mary Trail to the head of Cunningham Gulch as an alternate way out, assuming that you have a way of being picked up there. From the saddle next to Whitehead to Cunningham via the lakes is five miles, all downhill. (See the Highland Mary Lakes hike for details of that route.)

The return can be made by the approach route. The 13.2-mile round trip in the heading is based on this.

There is still another route. It swings south, then west around the base of Whitehead and back to Deer Park Trail. It is 1.8 miles further but is a more gradual trail. (Some might choose to follow it for the approach also.) To take it, follow the trail down the east side of the saddle as if going to Highland Mary Lakes. It starts south and a little east, then swings east. At a half mile, the trail divides; straight ahead goes to the lakes. A right turn takes you southwest along the base of the peak. In six-tenths mile you come to the Whitehead Trail. Take a right turn on it, and go west along the rim of Whitehead Gulch. After a mile, the trail swings northwest across Whitehead Mesa and in two miles comes back to the west end of Deer Park Basin; from here on, the route is the same as the approach. This route passes through a small strip of private property and mining areas.

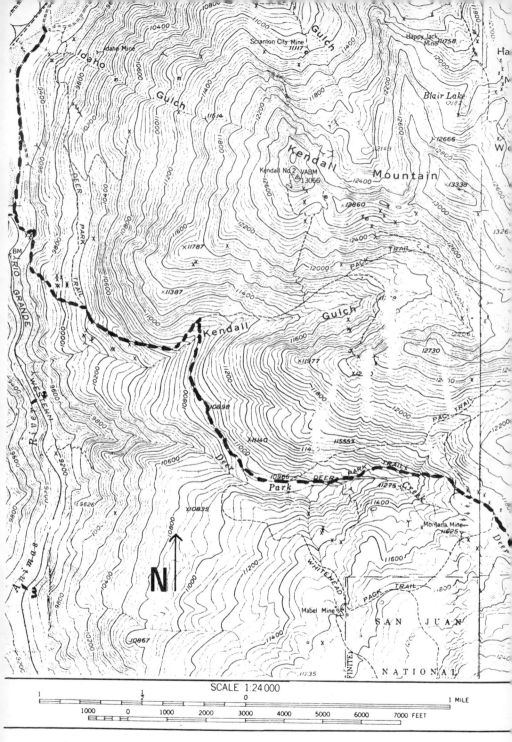

SCALE 1:24 000

1   ½   0   1 MILE

1000   0   1000   2000   3000   4000   5000   6000   7000 FEET

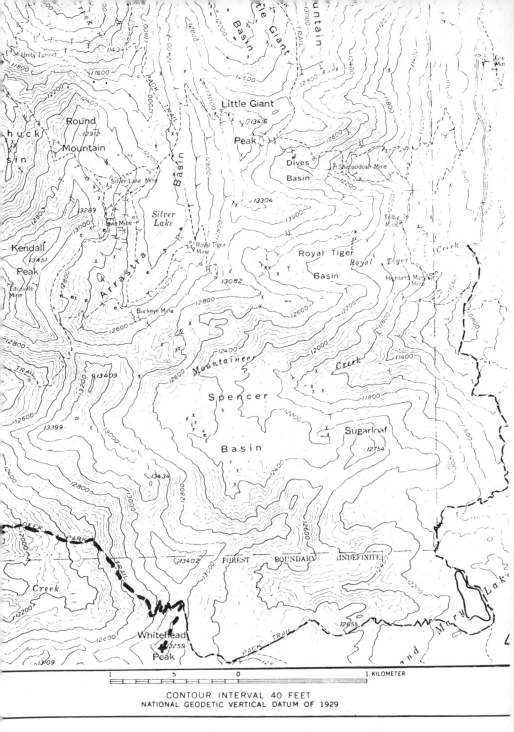

CONTOUR INTERVAL 40 FEET
NATIONAL GEODETIC VERTICAL DATUM OF 1929

Highland Mary Lakes

Distance: 6 miles (round trip)
Starting Elevation: 10,400 feet
Elevation Gain: 1,650 feet
High Point: 12,090 feet
Rating: Moderate to difficult
Time allowed: 3 to 5 hours
Maps: 7½ ' Howardsville
San Juan National Forest

Highland Mary Lakes is a favorite high-altitude area for fishing and for just being around water above timberline. The area has one large lake and several smaller ones. They are in a big tundra basin with a number of peaks visible around them.

To reach the lakes, go to the north end of Greene Street (the main street in Silverton), and turn right on Colorado State Route 110; follow this road four and one-fourth miles northeast to a right turn up Cunningham Gulch. Follow this road southeast four miles to its end at the head of the canyon. Along this route other roads turn off up the mountainside, but the main road stays near the bottom of the canyon near Cunningham Creek.

The hiking trail to the lakes starts at the head of the canyon on the west side of the creek and moves steadily uphill, crossing and recrossing the stream. In places it is muddy; much of it is rocky. It reaches the lakes in three miles.

The Verde Lakes are also worth visiting and lie one-half mile south of the southwest corner of the largest of the Highland Mary Lakes. There is a trail, but the Verde Lakes are easy to find anyway, since all this territory is open tundra above timberline. The Verde Lakes are only a hundred feet higher. A quarter mile south of Verde Lakes and a half mile west is still another accessible lake called Lost Lake. It is at about the same altitude.

The return from this hike is by the approach route. However, another option is to go west along a trail from the Highland Marys two miles over Whitehead Peak and back into Silverton via Deer Park Trail. (See the description just preceding this one.)

Highland Mary Lakes can also be approached from another route via Spencer Basin. For this one, go to the head of Cunningham Gulch as before, but follow an old mining road west up out of the gulch. Four-wheel-drive vehicles can make this road up into Spencer Basin about two miles up a series of switchbacks and across Mountaineer Creek to the south side of the basin. Out of the basin, hike south up 400 feet to a saddle. Over the saddle a little ways you can look eastward down on the Highland Mary Lakes. It is just over a one-mile hike to them; most of the way there is no trail, but this offers no problem except for short patches of brush.

Highland Mary Lakes from pass above Spencer Basin.

Highland Mary Lakes from pass above Spencer Basin.

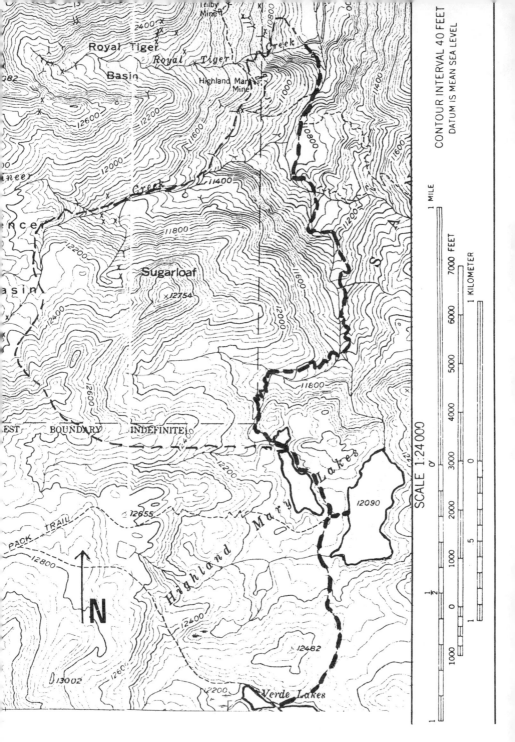

CONTOUR INTERVAL 40 FEET
DATUM IS MEAN SEA LEVEL

SCALE 1:24 000

175

Continental Divide

Distance: 15 miles (round trip)
Starting Elevation: 10,450 feet
Elevation gain: 2,390 feet
High Point: 12,840 feet
Rating: Difficult
Time Allowed: 10 to 13 hours
Maps: 7½ ' Howardsville
7½ ' Storm King
San Juan National Forest

This hike is rather ambitious for a one-day hike, but strong hikers can make it all right. The trip is well worthwhile, for it is one of the highest and most beautiful hikes in the state of Colorado. The continental divide raises its spiny back across the entire width of the state north to south; there are trails along it in several places. This particular chunk is east of Silverton, where much of the best in the San Juan Mountains can be seen. Fortunately, most of the ascent is made in the first three miles. After that, it rises only gradually for the most part.

To take this hike, go northeast out of Silverton to Cunningham Gulch and southeast to its terminus at the head of the canyon. (See the Highland Mary Lakes hike for a full description of this route.)

Start hiking south on the Highland Mary Lakes Trail. At four-tenths mile up this trail, another turns off to the left at the beginning of a flatter area. Take this route east and southeast another one and one-half miles to where another trail branches off to the right and moves southeast. This is the Continental Divide Trail. Follow this trail, which soon reaches the top of the divide and gradually ascends as it moves south along the ridge.

The projected hike goes five miles on south along the divide. At three and one-half miles, the trail divides. Keep to the right; the left trail descends the east side of the divide. Another half mile brings another choice; here, take the left trail. Another half mile brings you to a cross-trail; this is just over the highest point in the hike. A right turn here brings you to Eldorado Lake at 12,500 feet, the end point for this hike.

This is a long hike and beautiful all the way, but it could be shortened to some point short of Eldorado Lake at the discretion of the hiker.

Along the continental divide, the east side looks down into the headwaters of the Rio Grande River and into the Rio Grande National Forest. The west side looks into the Highland Mary Lakes Basin and, near the end of the hike, into the deep Elk Creek Canyon. But the most dramatic scenery is to the south and southwest, where rise the Grenadiers with many sharp and jagged peaks, their sheer cliffs plunging straight down along the north sides. Beyond the Grenadiers are the Needles. This is truly wild country!

The return trip can be made by the same route, but some of it can be varied. For this, go back along the same trail three and one-half miles, where there is a trail going west one and one-half miles to Verde Lakes. This trail does not show on the San Juan National Forest map. From Verde Lakes, go north two-thirds of a mile to Highland Mary Lakes, and pick up the trail between the two largest lakes. Follow it three miles as it winds around, generally moving north, back to your parking spot at the head of Cunningham Gulch.

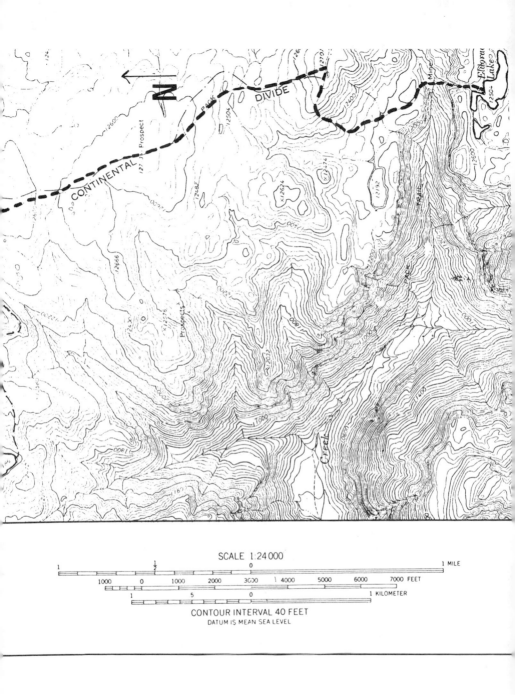

SCALE 1:24 000

CONTOUR INTERVAL 40 FEET
DATUM IS MEAN SEA LEVEL

Silver Lake

Distance: 2.5 miles (round trip)
Starting Elevation: 11,200 feet
Elevation Gain: 986 feet
High Point: 12,186 feet
Rating: Moderate
Time Allowed: 2 to 2 ½ hours
Maps: 7½ ' Howardsville
San Juan National Forest

Silver Lake is surrounded by many old mines. It is not good for fishing, because the water is highly mineralized from the mines, but it is a great place for mining buffs and bottle hunters.

To get to Silver Lake, take Colorado State Road 110 northeast out of Silverton two miles to a right turn downhill and across the Animas River. This brings you into Arrastra Gulch. It is 2.8 miles up this road to the parking place at the Mayflower Mine. There are several side roads where you can get lost. At the first split, take the left fork, which takes you up the side of the canyon a little ways and across the remains of an aerial tramway. Then the road turns right and parallels the tram above it for a half mile. Another road turns left in the middle of the half mile. Skip this one—it goes up to Little Giant Basin. The correct road continues paralleling the tramway and eventually crosses back to the right side of it. Then comes a switchback left and up. Two-wheel-drive vehicles should park here. This is above timberline. The fairly elaborate buildings of the Mayflower Mine are visible high above on the east side of the canyon. Hiking from here up the road to the mine adds a half mile of distance and 600 feet of vertical gain.

From the mine, a good trail leads south and a little east on up to the lake in a mile and a quarter, some of which is fairly steep.

The return is by the same route.

180

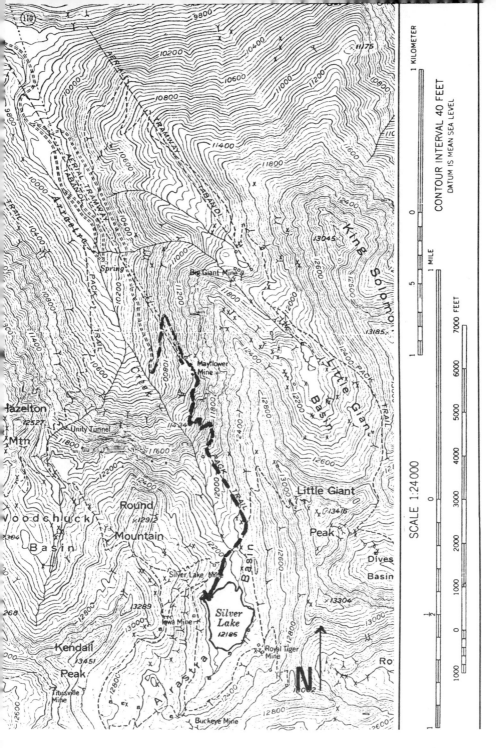

SCALE 1:24000

CONTOUR INTERVAL 40 FEET
DATUM IS MEAN SEA LEVEL

Mount Sneffels from Imogene Pass.

CHAPTER 7

The Area Fourteeners

Most people with some experience climbing in Colorado sooner or later get bitten by the "fourteener" bug. All of the highest mountains in Colorado are in this class. There are fifty-four mountains in the state above 14,000 feet but none higher than that. They start with Sunshine Peak at 14,001 feet and go to Mount Elbert at 14,433 feet, the highest in the state. Only Mount Whitney in California (of other peaks in the contiguous states) is taller, and even that is only by sixty-five feet). Geologically, the 14,000-foot bracket is the natural roof of the state.

These peaks present a unique challenge to the Colorado hiker; some of them are very difficult and are only for the thoroughly experienced climber. Others are not difficult at all; they are no more difficult than some lower climbs except that they present the problem of thin air. People with a history of heart trouble or high blood pressure should not attempt any of them without prior medical approval. For anyone else, a period of a few days of acclimatization at altitudes above 6,000 feet will be helpful. Or if a person has done some aerobic training, such as jogging or vigorous hiking at low altitude, he will likely be all right. Everyone at these higher levels experiences some shortness of breath. For the well trained, it only means slowing down some and taking more frequent (short) rests. Older people in good physical shape are not to be discouraged. I have climbed a number of these high peaks with some group members who are at or near retirement age. These people, in good condition, typically do well.

Twelve of the fifty-four fourteeners are located in southwest Colorado, the territorial limits of this book. They are: Handies, Redcloud, Sunshine, Wilson Peak, Mount Wilson, El Diente, Sunlight, Windom, Eolus, Sneffels, Wetterhorn, and Uncompahgre. I will describe the six of these that fit into the other limits set for this work: no technical climbing and no overnight backpacking. The other six involve more difficulty in climbing or overnight stays on the trail. Of the six described, some hikers may prefer to car camp for a night if they have had to drive some distance to the trail head, but none require the extra weight of sleeping equipment to be carried on the trail; day packs and canteens are adequate.

For those who want to branch out into other fourteeners anywhere in the state, I recommend two guidebooks for your consideration: Robert M. Ormes, *Guide to the Colorado Mountains,* Seventh Edition (1979), published by himself, and Walter R. Borneman and Lyndon J. Lampert, *A Climbing Guide to Colorado's Fourteeners* (1978), published by Pruett Publishing Company.

One other caution needs to be given for fourteeners:the snow problem. Unless you enjoy snow climbing and like to use crampons and ice axes, climbing in these mountains should be restricted to July through early September. Some years, snow conditions permit a little earlier and/or a little later climb. Even during the prime time, you may be called upon to cross some small snowfields. This requires extra care if they are steep. The extra care means kicking good solid steps or using an ice axe if the snow is too hard for steps. If you don't have an ice axe, you may be able to go around the snow above or below.

Mount Sneffels

Distance: 3 miles (round trip)
Starting Elevation: 12,400 feet
Elevation Gain: 1,750 feet
High Point: 14,150 feet
Rating: Moderate
Time Allowed: 3 to 4 hours
Maps: 7½' Mt. Sneffels
7½' Telluride
Uncompahgre National Forest

This is a fourteener but is fairly easy to climb by the route described below. The north face, however, is a challenge even for technical climbers. Since it is the highest point in the area, it commands tremendous views. I have found it especially rewarding in late September (if the snows have held off) during the season of aspen foliage color. The north and west sides of the mountain and the lower country to the south are mottled with gold mixed with the dark green of the high-altitude conifers. There is a long, wide valley to the north toward Ridgeway and Montrose, with Grand Mesa in the dim distance. Immediately to the south is St. Sophia Ridge, containing a half dozen or more peaks above 13,000 feet. Beyond that is lower timbered land, and still further are the San Miguels, with three fourteeners, and the unique shaft pointing skyward known as Lizard Head. The fourteeners here are Mount Wilson, Wilson Peak, and El Diente. East are the many, many high peaks of the San Juans.

The mileage and altitude gain given above depend upon four-wheel-drive transportation. Two-wheel drives will usually have to stop two miles and 1,600 feet further down. The hiking in these two miles is easy on the road.

To reach Sneffels, go to Ouray on U.S. Highway 550, seventy-five miles north of Durango and thirty-seven miles south of Montrose. The highway itself between Durango and Ouray is one of the most scenic in the state. It is called "the million-dollar highway" because of the gold ore in its base. It takes you over three passes that are 10,000 to 11,000 feet high. Sometimes you are riding on the edge of a sheer canyon wall. The twenty-five

185

miles between Silverton and Ouray are some of the most avalanche-prone stretches of highway in Colorado. Many avalanche paths run regularly each winter. Most have names. Riverside is a real killer, having snuffed out five lives in the last fifteen years. There is an institute in Silverton for avalanche study. Much is yet to be known about what causes them to run at certain times and not at others. When they do run, they have tremendous force. Riverside falls several thousand feet; in recent years, it has swept off the road and demolished both a bulldozer and a heavy snowplow truck, taking their operators to death in the process. The avalanche paths can be recognized by the clean stripes down the mountainsides where there are no trees, yet with heavy timber on either side. Early in the summer there will be large, hard piles of snow at the bottom containing tree branches.

Ouray is a picturesque little town nestled snugly in a small valley with high cliffs rising all around it. The town calls itself "The Switzerland of America." To go to Sneffels from Ouray, take the Camp Bird Mine road. It turns off U.S. Highway 550 just after the first switchback at the south end of town as the highway begins to rise. This is a good gravel road going southwest to the Camp Bird entrance. Here it curves around west and eventually northwest into Yankee Boy Basin. In a flat spot is the ghost town of Sneffels, with the ruins of its large ore-processing mill. Most buildings are down. Winters in the high country soon collapse unoccupied buildings due to the very heavy snow load.

Yankee Boy Basin is a beautiful valley with many wild flowers and a lovely waterfall.

Beyond Camp Bird, the road begins to get rough, and two-wheelers have to stop soon. After a fairly level spot just above timberline, the road climbs very steeply and ends up moving north on the north side of the basin. There is adequate parking here, but you should not move out onto the tundra with a vehicle, since the tundra is very fragile and scars can last many years.

From the parking place, hike west across talus through a relatively flat area for three-quarters of a mile. There is a fairly good trail most of this way, which speeds up talus walking. At this point, you will come to a wide couloir or chute. Follow it north up a steep slope to a saddle. This will be fairly difficult climbing, because the scree on the slope makes you slip regularly. Often it is easier to step out of the main path and climb on rocks that are a little larger. The scree is great for a rapid, shuffling descent. At the saddle, turn west (left), and ascend another

186

Looking down the rocky chute on Mount Sneffels showing the saddle below.

Looking down on Blue Lakes from the top of Mount Sneffels. A good example of a rock glacier is on the left.

steep couloir; this one is filled with big rocks that you have to climb over and around. Just below the top of this, climb out the south side and on up the cone to the summit. There is a pretty well-worn route that you can follow easily. There is some exposure here, but it is not really dangerous if you move with care. The top is very small and can only accommodate a few people at a time. The wind is usually calm on this peak; you can enjoy the views and relax after the steep climb in comfort.

The descent is made by the same route as the climb. The

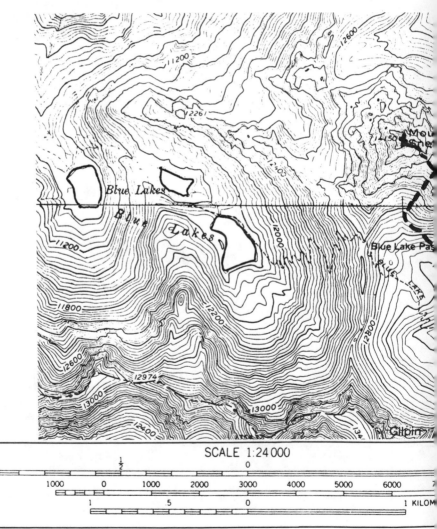

SCALE 1:24 000

scree becomes fun on the way down.

On the south side of the mountain is a small north-south ridge, substantially below the summit separating Yankee Boy Basin from the Blue Lakes area. I feel confident you could return by this way, if you wish to vary the route, but I have not tried it. If you park where I have suggested for four-wheel drives, it would lengthen the return and involve some ascent back to your car. There is a trail in this area that leads back down the basin.

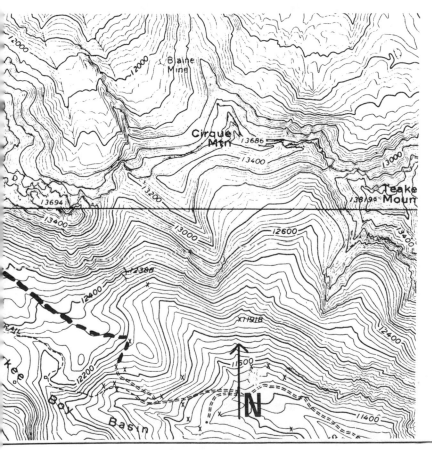

1 MILE

FEET

CONTOUR INTERVAL 40 FEET
DATUM IS MEAN SEA LEVEL

Wilson Peak

Distance: 8 miles (round trip)
Starting Elevation: 10,500 feet
Elevation Gain: 3,517 feet
High Point: 14,017 feet
Rating: Difficult
Time Allowed: 5 to 6 hours
Maps: 7½ ' Dolores Peak
7½ ' Mount Wilson
Uncompahgre National Forest

Wilson Peak is one of three fourteeners in the San Miguel Mountains; as fourteener climbs go, it is not among the easiest but is easier than average. The other two in the group are Mount Wilson and El Diente ("the tooth" in Spanish); these two are much too difficult to fit into the scope of this guide. Both are quite hard at the top, and the ridge between them is known as one of the toughest in the state. But Wilson Peak can be climbed by anyone of durability and some rock scrambling experience.

This is an area that has had a great deal of mining activity in the past, and some is going on now.

I will describe the Silver Pick route. This is not the only route, but is the shortest.

The approach is made from Highway 145 between Placerville and Telluride. About seven miles southeast of the Placerville junction of Highways 62 and 145 are the remains of the town of Vanadium. A dirt road turns south off the highway here, crosses the San Miguel River, and follows up Bear Creek. (Don't make the mistake of turning off further west at the Fall Creek turnoff.)

On the Bear Creek Road there are some possible turnoff roads; generally speaking, choose straight ahead at these options. Currently, there are signs; choose those marked for Silver Pick. The distance from the highway to the Wilson Mountains Primitive Area barrier is about seven and one-half miles. There is a good parking and small camping area to the left of the road just before the barrier. Park or car camp here. The last three to four miles of road are all right when dry for two-wheel drives but

Wilson Peak looking northeast across Navajo Basin from El Diente Peak. The trail comes across the saddle around and up the right side of the peak.

require four-wheel drives when wet. The rest of the road is good gravel.

Hiking starts up the same road beyond the barrier. At about a mile and a quarter, an old mill appears on the right with one building in rather good condition. Just before the building, the main road switches back left; follow it. After the next switchback, go about another quarter mile to where the trail starts up steeply. It is small and easily missed, but once on it, you will find it unmistakable. You could follow the road, but it is much longer and less interesting.

After climbing about 500 feet, you will be over the first hump of rocks and will be able to see the top of Wilson Peak straight ahead. To the right of it is a saddle at 13,000 feet. A little further on, the trail divides, the left side going straight for the peak. The last 1,000 feet this way climb a steep couloir directly below the peak, which can be quite hazardous for the novice. The right fork of this trail is easier. It winds its way up to the saddle. On the way up on a little plateau are the remains of the old "hotel," a remarkably well-built stone structure where miners could sleep and eat far above timberline in the old days.

From the saddle there is a fairly distinct trail climbing east around the south end of the descending Wilson Peak ridge. Once around, climb northeast to the summit, staying just below

Lizard Head.

The "Hotel" below Wilson Peak.

the ridge on the east side until near the top. A short descent takes you over to the west side briefly in an exposed area, where some careful scrambling must be done. The top is just ahead.

From the top, the rest of the San Miguels are the near scene. Gladstone is southwest of Wilson Peak; the two are tied together by a narrow, rocky ridge. Gladstone, at 13,913 feet, just misses the fourteener class, but it is a tougher climb than Wilson Peak. The west side of Gladstone is marked by a deep gash that separates it from Mount Wilson; here lies one of the few glaciers in this part of the state. On the west side of the gash is a very high and rough ridge. Mount Wilson peaks out at the east end of it and El Diente at the west end. They are both great climbs but only for experienced climbers, or at least for parties with experienced leadership. The exposures at and near the top are awesome.

In the view to the southeast, the eye is immediately caught by Lizard Head, a shaft of rock rising 400 feet straight up out of the top of the mountain.

To the west is Dolores Peak and, still further, Lone Cone. Beyond this radius to the north, east, and south are many high peaks too numerous to detail here. They display well the ruggedness of southwestern Colorado.

The return route from Wilson Peak is the same as the approach.

Another route for the climb deserves mention, but not full description. The starting and parking point is a little dirt road that turns west off Highway 145 about one and one-half miles south of the top of Lizard Head Pass. This route passes by the base of the Lizard Head shaft and into Bilk Basin for the ascent of Wilson Peak. This route is long and requires packing in overnight gear.

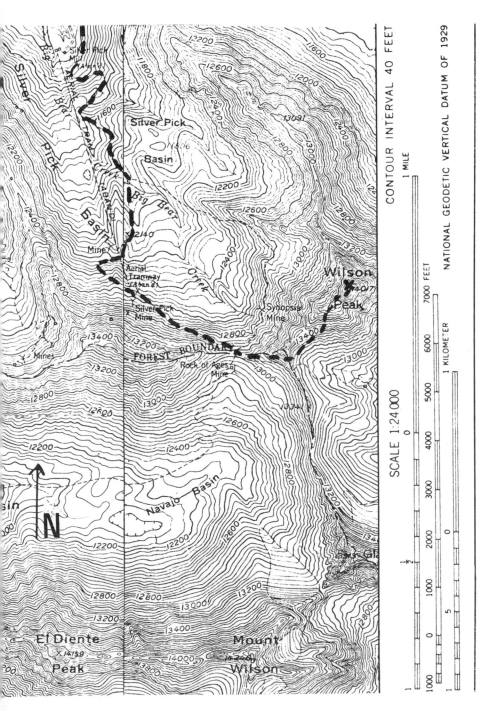

SCALE 1:24 000

CONTOUR INTERVAL 40 FEET

NATIONAL GEODETIC VERTICAL DATUM OF 1929

Handies Peak

Distance: 3 miles (round trip)
Starting Elevation: 11,800 feet
Elevation Gain: 2,248 feet
High Point: 14,048 feet
Rating: Moderate
Time Allowed: 3 to 4 hours
Maps: 7½ ' Handies Peak
7½ ' Redcloud Peak

As fourteeners go, Handies is an easy one; it is rated a moderate hike only because of the altitude. But it is rewarding,
because its summit provides an unrestricted view in all directions. Skylines are tremendous, better than that of any city in the
world, for there are hundreds of high peaks visible on a clear
day, typical of the summer forenoons.

Handies is in a remote area. From Durango, you must go
fifty miles on U.S. Highway 550 to Silverton, eight miles on
rough gravel to Animas Forks, and seven miles on a very rough
four-wheel-drive road to the start of the climb. Hikers with only
two-wheel-drive vehicles will need to approach from the east via
Colorado State Highway 149 through Lake City. I will describe
the Silverton route first.

At the north end of Silverton's Greene Street (the main
street of the town), turn right and follow Colorado State
Road 110. This starts as pavement but soon turns to gravel. Follow this road about eight miles to a division, where the
left side leads down along the river to the ghost town of Animas
Forks visible a half mile ahead. You should take the right fork
uphill and shift into four-wheel drive. In less than a half mile, the
Cinnamon Pass Road turns off very sharply and steeply uphill to
the right; it is so sharp that vehicles with longer wheel bases have
to go past the turn, turn around in the road, and come back to it.
This is a picturesque road above timberline, with high peaks and
deep canyons to impress you with nature's ability at sculpturing.
There are also many wild flowers along the way, including the
beautiful columbine, Colorado's state flower. Two and one-half

196

High cliffs at the head of American Basin. Just below these turn left to climb Handies Peak.

miles up this road you top out at the pass at 12,600 feet. It is worth a stop here to look around and to thank your vehicle for having made it. Just over two miles down the other side, shortly after entering timber again, as you are rounding a left-turn switchback, a road turns off sharply to the right, downhill. There should be a sign indicating "American Basin." Take this road as far as you can (about two miles). Park off the road, and prepare to climb. The altitude and hiking distance given in the heading for this hike are relative, depending on how far up this road you are brave enough to drive. Two miles will get you to 12,400 feet. The 11,800-foot mark given is only about 1.2 miles.

For the Lake City route, turn south along the west side of the valley about one and one-half miles southeast of the town of Lake City. This soon brings you along beautiful Lake San Cristobal. Beyond the lake, the road climbs several hundred feet above the Lake Fork of the Gunnison River and becomes the "shelf road," beautiful in its vistas, but steep and narrow in its traverse. Beyond the shelf, the road enters a more comfortable valley. As you are about to make the first switchback to start up Cinnamon Pass, you will come to the American Basin turnoff on the left. If you are in a two-wheel-drive car, you can still get part way up this road, though it gets rough fairly soon.

The hiking route: As you face south to the head of American Basin, you will see it walled off with high, broken cliffs, awesome bastions protecting the valley. Move in this direction until you come to a little side stream descending from Sloan Lake high above. Follow east southeast to a marshy, near-level area. At this point, turn northeast and attack the mountain proper. There is a trail in some places both before and after this area, but mostly the climb to the summit will be on open, steep, and rocky tundra.

As you get up to about 13,200 feet, you will be able to look back south and see Sloan Lake, nestled in its well-guarded surroundings. The lake is bigger than it appears at first sight, containing several acres of cold trout water. It is worth a side trip on the way down.

In only a half mile of the steep climb, you are rewarded with the summit cairn. The top is fairly broad and relatively smooth. There is a steep drop-off northeastward into Grizzly Gulch. Looking across this into and up the other side of the Lake Fork Valley to the massif, you will see Redcloud and Sunshine. Further north on the horizon, you can see two more fourteeners— Wetterhorn (14,015 feet) and Uncompahgre (14,300 feet). To the west and a bit north, Sneffels (14,150 feet) should be the highest point on the skyline. To the south is a great host of other San Juan peaks.

The return trip is by the same route, although you could come straight west down the steep side of the mountain, taking care to avoid the few cliffs that are there.

An alternate route up Handies is directly out of the Lake Fork Valley up Grizzly Gulch. There is an old trail four miles to the top, starting at 10,400 feet and producing a total gain of 3,648 feet.

198

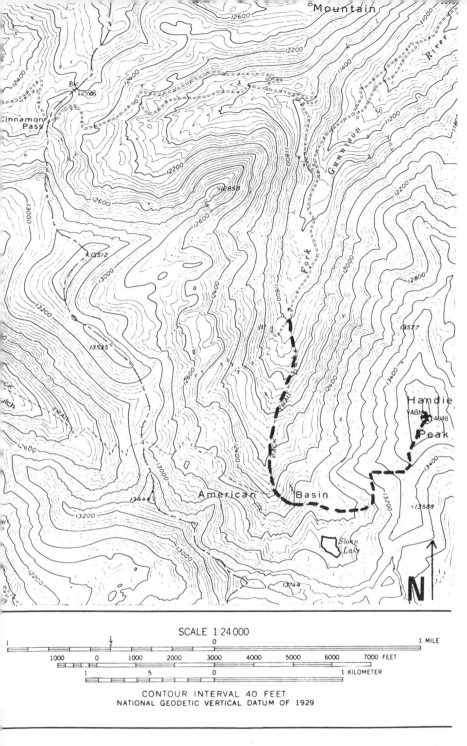

SCALE 1:24 000

CONTOUR INTERVAL 40 FEET
NATIONAL GEODETIC VERTICAL DATUM OF 1929

Redcloud and Sunshine

Distance: 9.7 miles (round trip)
Starting Elevation: 10,400 feet
Elevation Gain: 4,134 feet (includes
  500 feet lost and regained)
High Point: 14,034 feet
Rating: Difficult
Time Allowed: 6 to 7 hours
Maps: 7½ ' Redcloud Peak

Redcloud and Sunshine are two fourteeners that are usually climbed together. There is a 500-foot drop to the saddle between which is all that has to be regained to get the second peak on the same trip. So here is a fairly easy way to bag two fourteeners in one day. In fact, they are close enough to Handies that strong parties, bent on making fast time, could do all three in one day. The rating of difficult is given because of the distance and total altitude gain, which are enough to tire even practiced climbers. However, there is no really difficult spot anywhere along this route. The distance on the round trip can be cut nearly two miles and the elevation gain reduced nearly 800 feet for those with four-wheel drive.

To reach the trail head, follow the same directions from Silverton or Lake City given for Handies Peak, except go to where Silver Creek crosses the Lake Fork Valley Road. The trail head is four miles downstream from the American Basin turnoff; it is where Grizzly and Silver Creek both come into Lake Fork. For those with four-wheel drive, turn northeast off the road here and follow a jeep trail to its terminus in about one mile. There is parking here for one to three vehicles. Others should hike up the jeep trail.

The trail head starts northeast at the edge of a clearing right near the parking spot and almost immediately crosses a little side stream where the water is cool and usually safe to drink. The trail quickly emerges above timberline and follows the left side of Silver Creek about two miles, eventually crossing it and spiraling up the back side of Redcloud southward to a saddle at 13,000 feet. At this point, the trail dips down the other side.

Abandon it; turn right and climb southeast up a ridge to its top. Here, turn south and hike an easy two-tenths mile to the summit. Standing on the top, feast your eyes on peaks and valleys galore. The views are much the same as described for Handies, except that Sunshine looms large in the southern vista.

Marmots inhabit much of the backcountry high altitudes (9,000 feet or less and up). They are furry rodents with bushy tails and weigh about eight pounds. Because of their whistlelike call, they are nicknamed "whistle pigs." They like to sit up on their hind legs and stare at you or peek from behind a rock. Sometimes you can get within a few feet of them, but usually they quickly duck into a nearby hole that they have kept conveniently close to.

From Redcloud, it is an easy mile and a half south down into a saddle and out again up to the top of Sunshine.

For the return trip, some distance can be saved by going back north to the saddle and angling northwest down the side of Redcloud. This will take you to the south fork of Silver Creek, which rises in a large basin on the west side of Redcloud. The descent to the basin is talus but not difficult. The bottom of the basin is quite irregular. Exercising some care and keeping mostly to the right side of the stream will pay off in easier hiking. At or near timberline, you should find a trail that will take you the rest of the way down to Silver Creek and back to your parking spot.

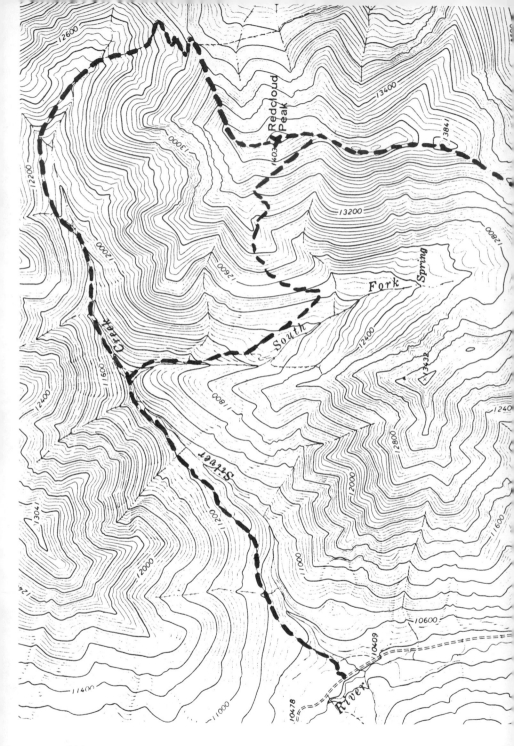

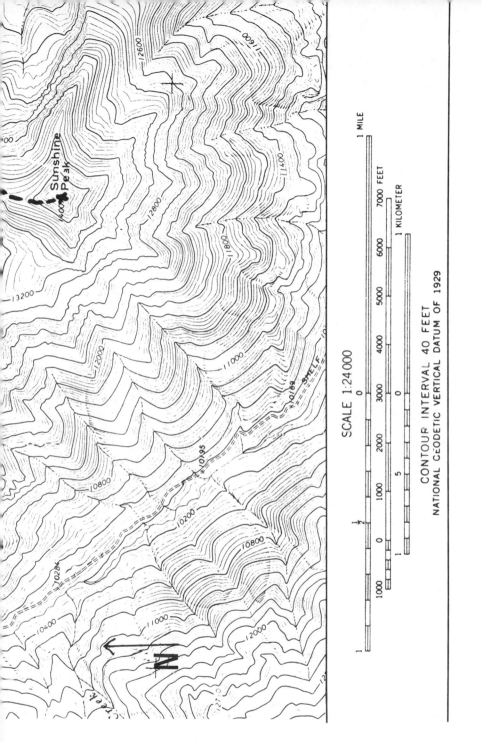

SCALE 1:24 000

CONTOUR INTERVAL 40 FEET
NATIONAL GEODETIC VERTICAL DATUM OF 1929

Uncompahgre Peak, Matterhorn, Wetterhorn

Distance: 16 miles (round trip)
Starting Elevation: 11,000 feet
Elevation Gain: 4,309 feet
High Point: 14,309 feet
Rating: Moderate
Time Allowed: 7 to 8 hours
Maps: 7½' Uncompahgre
7½' Wetterhorn Peak
Uncompahgre National Forest

Uncompahgre Peak is a fourteener, one of the easiest in the state to climb, but the hike is quite long. As with all the four-teeners, it stands out above most of its surroundings; so the view from the top is certainly rewarding. Actually, it is the highest point in southwestern Colorado and the sixth highest peak in the state. The rating is moderate not because there are any diffi-culties, but only because of the altitude and length of the hike.

Uncompahgre has a very distinctive top that can easily be recognized from the east, the west, and the south. The top is very large and relatively smooth compared to most high peaks, being something close to 300 yards long and 100 yards wide and gently sloping to the southeast. This is the approach for the climb. The north face is, however, a complete contrast, plunging straight down nearly 1,000 feet. It is awesome!

The hike described here is the easy but long route.

Uncompahgre is in real backcountry. It is approached via a little road between Silverton and Lake City. From Lake City, take Henson Creek Road west out of town, and follow the creek to Capitol City nine miles west. This is a two-wheel-drive road.

The route from Silverton is over Engineer Pass, a four-wheel-drive road. Go northeast off the north end of Greene Street (the main street) out of Silverton. Follow this to the branch off to the right and uphill one-half mile south of Animas Forks. This is where the four-wheel drive begins. Follow this north 4.8 miles to the top of Engineer Pass (12,800 feet). There is some beautiful country to be surveyed from the top of the pass,

Uncompahgre Peak from the west showing its large flat top. The main trail goes around the right end. The shortcut through the steep notch is seen as a light streak of rocks half way down the right side.

including the deep valley into which you are about to descend. It is nine miles down the east side of the pass to Capitol City.

Capitol City is a ghost town with a few buildings still standing in the largest flat spot in Henson Creek Valley. Its mining founders of a hundred years ago were ambitious and dreamed of replacing Denver as the capital.

At Capitol City, take a side road northwest two miles along the North Fork of Henson Creek to Matterhorn Creek. Turn right here, and drive as far as you can. A mile up this road is a vehicle barrier where all cars must stop; two-wheel drives may have to stop a little short of this spot. If you want to car camp, there are a few places along this way flat enough to use.

Hiking starts up the same road and soon gets above timberline. Stay to the right of the creek. As you reach higher ground in the openness of the tundra, you can begin to see the three high peaks of the area. Wetterhorn (14,015 feet) is to the left; Matterhorn (13,590 feet) is almost straight ahead; Uncompahgre, our objective, is off to the right.

Follow the trail to a saddle between Matterhorn and Uncompahgre, taking the right-hand side where the trails come in from the north. The Uncompahgre Trail swings back southeast for one and one-half miles beyond the saddle, joins a trail there going north another mile, and joins still another trail that ascends the southeast ridge, at first westerly and then northwesterly another mile to the top. This is a long, gradual, easy route.

An alternative route can cut off as much as two miles but is much steeper. It is worth it to many hikers for the time saved. At the Matterhorn-Uncompahgre saddle where the trail starts southeast, abandon it, and strike out northeast toward the mountain itself. There are two ways it can be climbed from the west side, neither of which is a trail. There is a large notch one-half mile south of the summit filled with steep talus. The route works quite well, though some of the rocks near the top are loose enough to require some care. Once over the top of this, on the solid again, you will find the trail ascending from the southeast. Join it for an easy half mile to the top—not too easy, though, for it includes another 900 feet of altitude gain.

The other west side way is north of this notch and the large cliffs near it. Choose a route far enough to the left of these cliffs

Wetterhorn Peak from the shoulder of Matterhorn.

On Wetterhorn's last steep pitch with a fixed safety rope.

to aim for a point just south of the top, where there is a break in the last two bands of summit cliffs. This route is quite steep, but it will work all right. You will be on tundra part of the time and loose rock part of the time. It is the fastest route from the west side. The last time I climbed in this area, a friend and I used this route; it was short enough that we were able to climb Uncompahgre, Matterhorn, and Wetterhorn all in one day. This would not have been possible using either of the other routes.

Once on top, you are "king of the mountain," for this is the highest point in the area, and you can see many miles in all directions on a good day, and vast stretches of peaks and big valleys. The nearest peaks, of course, are Matterhorn, which you can now look down on, and Wetterhorn. To the north of Wetterhorn is Coxcomb, so named because of the appearance of its unique top.

The descent is best made by the approach route. One of the others given here would work, but the two west side routes are hard to pick out from above if you did not come up one of them.

Strong parties who are intent on "peak bagging" can climb one or both of the other two peaks in the group in the same day, assuming they are qualified. Matterhorn is no problem. It can be

Matterhorn Peak as seen across the sharp connecting ridge from Wetterhorn.

climbed by bushwhacking up the southeast side on the way back from Uncompahgre. It is steep tundra at first; this gives way to large rocks—some loose, some fixed—as you get within 500 or 600 feet from the top. In some locations, Matterhorn would be an impressive peak, but here it is subdued by its two higher neighbors. The most impressive view here is the ridge on the west side connecting to Wetterhorn. This is a jagged knife edge a mile long. Just looking at it can be scary.

Wetterhorn is not recommended for novices without experienced leadership, for the last sixty feet or more are very steep. There are good small toeholds and handholds, but unfortunately, many of these are covered with sand and gravel, giving a very treacherous surface. A fixed rope in this area is a good idea as a safety feature.

For those who want to climb Wetterhorn after doing Matterhorn and/or Uncompahgre, the following route is recommended. Drop down below Matterhorn to the southwest to about 12,600 feet, and go west to the ridge running southeast from Wetterhorn. You could stay higher near the connecting ridge, but this is not profitable because it is so full of big boulders that it makes tedious, slow going. Mount straight up the southeast ridge; at the top, strike northwest toward the summit. There is a well-worn path most of this way. At about 100 feet below the summit is a very nice pocket big enough to accommodate a good-sized party. There is a high wall on the west side and good shelter from wind all the way around. It makes a fine rest and snack stopping place. The top of Wetterhorn is much smaller than that of Uncompahgre. The north side, like Uncompahgre, is a sheer drop.

For the descent, go back down the southeast ridge about a mile, and drop off the east side. (The south end has cliffs that cannot be interpreted very well from above.) Across the stream at the bottom, you should soon pick up the trail that you came up earlier in the day for the return to your parking place.

The mileage and rating given in the heading are for Uncompahgre only. If Matterhorn and Wetterhorn are done also, add 2.8 more miles and 2,500 feet more of ascent. The rating in this case would be hard.

Columbine, the Colorado State flower, growing out of a crack in a vertical rock.

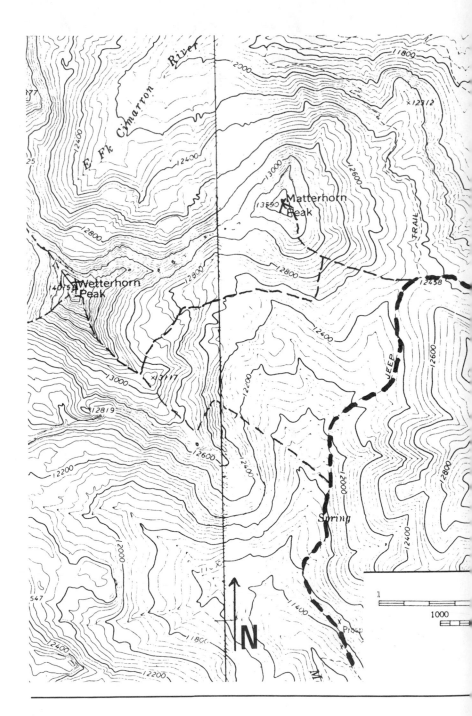

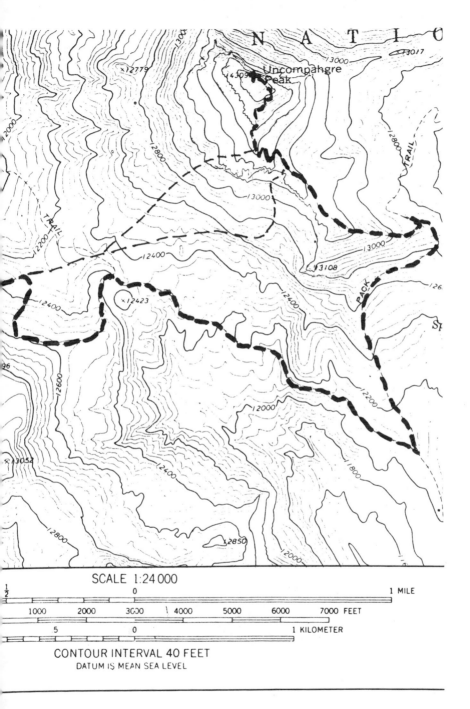

NATIO

13017

×12779

13000

Uncompahgre
Peak

TRAIL

12800

12800

TRAIL

12800

13000

13000

12200

12400

13108

126.

12400

×12423

2400

PACK

St

96

12600

12200

×13054

12400

12000

1800

12800

12850

2000

SCALE 1:24 000

½

0   1 MILE

1000   2000   3000   4000   5000   6000   7000 FEET

5   0   1 KILOMETER

CONTOUR INTERVAL 40 FEET
DATUM IS MEAN SEA LEVEL

Index

Animas City Mountain 15-19

Banded Mountain 72, 75
Barnroof Point 22-24
Burnt Timber Trail 52-54

Cascade Creek 117, 119, 120,
  125, 147-153
Chicago Basin 48, 106
Clear Lake 157, 162-164
Centennial Peak 74-78
Cinnamon Pass 196-197
Coal Creek 124-127
Continental Divide 176-179
Crater Lake 131-135

Deadwood Mountain 68-70
Deer Creek 124-127
Dear Park Trail 168-171, 172
Diorite Peak 71-73
Dry Creek 25-26
Durango City Reservoir 53
Dutch Creek 90-91, 96

Elbert Creek 98-100
Emerald Lake 47
Emergencies 9-11

Engineer Mountain 115-118,
  149
Equipment 11-13

First Fork 42, 55, 57
Fort Lewis College 27, 29, 76
Four Base Lake 101-102
Fuller Lake 157, 160

Gibbs Peak 85-87
Goulding Creek 95-97
Grand Turk Mountain 128-130
Grant, U.S. 161
Graysill-Grayrock 140-142
Grizzly Peak 119-123

Haflin Creek 41-43
Handies Peak 196-199
Haviland Lake 101
Hermosa Peak 143-146
Hermosa Trail 89-91
Hesperus Mountain 78-81
Highland Mary Lakes 169, 172-
  175, 176-177
Hogsback 20-23, 35

Ice Lakes 157-161

213

Island Lake 157, 160-161

Jones Creek 93, 96
Jura Knob 124-127

Kendall Mountain 165-167, 168
Kennebec Pass 62-66

Lake Hope 154-156
Lost Lake 172

Maps 6-7
Matterhorn Peak 204-211
Missionary Ridge 41-61
Mitchell Lakes 92-94
Molas Trail 103-105, 106
Mount Baker 62, 68-70
Mountain View Crest 46-51
Mount Sneffels 185-189

Overlook Point 47

Parrott Peak 82-84
Pear Lake 47
Perins City 31, 38
Perins Peak 34-39
Potato Hill 109, 113-114
Potato Lake 109-111
Purgatory Trail 106-108

Raider Ridge 27-29
Rating System 4-6
Redcloud Peak 198, 200-203

Redcreek 42, 55-58
Rock glaciers 116, 187
Ruby Lake 47

Sharkstooth 74-78
Shearer Creek 42, 56, 59-61
Silver Lake 180-181
Silver Mountain 67-70
Snowdon Peak 136-139
South Mineral Creek 125, 147-153, 155, 157, 162
Spud Lake 109-111
Spud Mountain 109, 113-114
Sultan Mountain 128-130
Sunshine Peak 198, 200-203

Taylor Lake 62, 63-64
Time estimates 6
Tomahawk Basin 71-73
Transfer Park 53, 54
Twilight Peaks 131-135
Twin Buttes 31-33

Uncompahgre Peak 198, 204-211
U.S. Grant Peak 161

Verde Lakes 172, 175, 177

Wallace Lake 44-45
Webb Lake 47
Wetterhorn Peak 198, 204-211
Whitehead Peak 168-171, 172
Wilson Peak 190-195